Writing as a Second Language

Writing as a Second Language

From Experience to Story to Prose

DONALD DAVIS

AUGUST HOUSE PUBLISHERS, INC.
LITTLE ROCK

Published 2000 by August House, Inc.,
P.O. Box 3223, Little Rock, Arkansas, 72203,
501-372-5450

Printed in the United States of America
9 8 7 6 5 4 3 2

Library of Congress Cataloging-in-Publication Data
Davis, Donald, 1944–
Writing as a second language : from experience to story to prose
/ Donald Davis.
        p.   cm.
ISBN 0-87483-567-4 (pbk. : alk. paper)
1. English language—Rhetoric. 2. Written communication.
3. Oral communication. 4. Report writing. 5. Storytelling. I. Title.
PE1408.D2385 2000
808'.042—dc21   00-032771

Copy Editor: Tom Baskett
Production Editor: Joy Freeman
Cover Design: Byron Taylor
Interior Design: Joy Freeman and David Fowlkes

The paper used in this publication meets the
minimum requirements of the American National
Standard for Information Sciences—Permanence of Paper
for Printed Library Materials, ANSI Z39.48-1984.

AUGUST HOUSE   PUBLISHERS   LITTLE ROCK

This book is dedicated to:

Judy Conklin

Mary Jean Smith

Patty Smith

Evelyn Jordan

and

Joyce Morgan,
unique and dedicated educators
whose work has greatly enriched the lives
of all those whom they have met.

Part One:
Developing a Workable Model for Language

Part Two:
Developing a Workable Model for Writing

Appendices

Writing as a Second Language

Developing a Workable Model for Language

ONE

A New Look at Teaching Language

It all started on a very hot day in September. School had been in session for less than two weeks, and, as visiting author and storyteller, I was already making my third visit of the year. The school was in Georgia, and the temperature inside the building, one of those dinosaurs from the days when no one could imagine air conditioning in schools, was at least in the high 80s, with ample humidity to hold the heat firmly in place.

I checked in at the main office and had my preliminary meeting with the school principal. We reviewed the schedule for the day, the principal apologized for the heat, and we left the office together to walk to the library where I would be turned over to the librarian, my host and guide for Visiting Author's Day.

Because of the heat, every window and door of the school was propped open, and every available fan had been pressed into service. As the principal and I walked down the long hall, we could over-hear everything that was happening in the class-rooms along the way.

As we approached one particular fifth-grade room, more than the usual amount of talking seemed to be coming through the open door. Suddenly, from inside the classroom, we heard the teacher take charge.

"Stop talking!" Her voice rolled out from the door. "Stop talking...you're supposed to be working on *language!*"

The principal and I both stopped in our tracks and laughed. Then we quickly went on to the library, and I fulfilled my residency for the day.

Later in the evening, I was talking with friends about what had happened that day. When I remembered the "working on language" incident, it hit me more deeply than before. Suddenly I realized that what the school principal and I had overheard was somehow deeper than a momentary joke.

Over time, I continued to reflect on my many experiences visiting schools. As I thought through my work as a traveling "school watcher," what had happened that day bored deeply into my mind. I soon realized that though we talk about teaching *language arts* in school, we do not often teach the wholeness of our language arts. No, over and over, I see people actually teaching only *reading and writing* instead of nurturing the whole sweep of the rich oral and kinesthetic package that is our most beautiful, most utilitarian language.

What I had experienced on that day—"Stop talking, you're supposed to be working on language"—hit me in the head. And the concussion has lingered. Through my work in schools, I see more and more a strong emphasis on the written *product* as sole measure of language development. With equal frequency, I hear teachers and administrators complain about their difficulty in pulling writing from their students. I am asked again and again to talk with students about writing and about how they might get ideas for their own writing. These requests are usually accompanied by teachers' laments over their failures to inspire writing in their students.

After that September day in the Georgia school, I began to wonder if our difficulty in teaching *writing* could come from our failure to acknowledge and work with the wholeness of our language. When we teach writing *directly* and *separately* from that wholeness, are we just patching holes in the visible roof of our house of language while crumbling foundations threaten to topple the house itself?

In thinking about this subject, I have begun to ask several questions, not theoretically, but through my own observations and work with thousands of students: What is language, anyway? How is it developed, nurtured, and maintained through the course of perpetual and lifelong growth? What are the roles of writing in the overall shape of our language package? Can writing be approached separately, or must it be part of a more holistic treatment of our language-development process? Dozens of other questions have followed, and this book documents my grappling with them.

The real point of this work is to thaw frozen writers, but the process is one that begins with understanding our functional language itself. My goal is to see a remodeling of basic approaches, not a bandaging of old ones.

In short, we will be getting to a new model for teaching that views writing as the final stage of life-language development. But we will not start there. First we will look at definitions: what language is as a whole and how it is born, developed, and nurtured. Then we will come to the purpose for it all—a new and more holistic way to *do the write thing!*

TWO

A New Look at Functional Language Development

Humans come into the world as incomplete creations. We arrive in this life in "kit form," and much of our lives is spent in being put (and putting ourselves) together. One part of humanness that we come into the world *without* is our functional language. Acquiring it takes time.

The process of language development continues throughout our entire lives. Yet we often divide it artificially into several distinct "steps" or acquisition levels.

The "step" metaphor is problematic in and of itself. No matter how much we try to talk our way out of it, the visual metaphor of "steps in the development process" contains an inherent danger. When we walk up steps, we leave each behind forever as we ascend to the next. No one can stand on each and every step all at once, yet that is exactly what we must do in effective language development. For that reason we will not speak here of "steps" or "stages" but rather try a different visual model that seems more appropriate in understanding how language develops.

We will be looking at four sequentially added dimensions of functional language development. But since each dimension *must be maintained* rather than left behind as we move along, "braiding the cable" will be our metaphor for picturing language development.

In "braiding" anything, we begin with a single strand that is not used and left behind, but instead is strengthened by having an additional strand *added to it*. After that, a third strand may be added and, with our language model, a fourth.

For a cable to hang together, the first strand must run the full length along with each and every strand as it gets added. In fact, if any one strand is allowed to drop out, the entire cable falls apart and fails to function.

This visual image is very important as we look at language development. We are *not* looking at sequentially attained and then abandoned steps, but rather at added dimensions that must always be maintained. With this metaphor strongly in mind, let us proceed to examine the four progressive dimensions of functional language development.

The Progressively Braided Cable of Functional Language

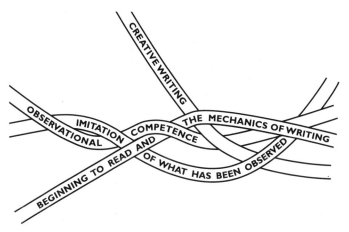

The Initial Dimension (first strand): Observational Competence

All language growth (and perhaps all learning of every sort) is based on modeling. Modeling cannot work effectively, however, until the learner acquires a competent level of observational fluency.

Sometimes what we are discussing here has been called "listening skill." However, it goes far beyond mere listening. Observational competence does involve good listening, but it also requires careful, analytical watching, attention to the senses of taste and smell, and developed tactile contact with the world. All five of our observational senses must be well exercised to the extent of our physical abilities. If, for example, hearing is missing from our observational arsenal, other senses must compensate.

Observational competence also involves one's own feelings toward the information taken in. Such interpretive feelings as love and hate, fear and safety, and liking and disliking modify both the form and content of the information our senses detect.

Besides feelings, our deductive and inductive reasoning skills modify and interpret the relationship between what the senses take in and the flowing course of life around us. All these things go together to make up an observational package that begins developing at birth and never stops nurturing our language.

Let us look at a simple example of observational competence in the very young child. He or she is constantly surrounded by sensory input, most of which seems at first to be random and unorganized. However, as observational skill becomes greater, patterns start to emerge. For example, something in the child's mind begins to notice that his or her crying often provokes the caretaking adult to make the same sound: "Bottle?" Then, what is later labeled as "bottle" gets offered to the baby's mouth, and the crying stops. This activity often is accompanied by pleasant touching and cuddling, and the "bottle" contains something satisfying both in its taste and in its bulk!

It may not be possible for the younger child (or indeed the adult) to verbalize the content of all observations. These are, however, needed in order for the next developmental dimension (strand) to be braided into our cable of language.

It already has been noted, but should be stressed, that children who lack one or more operating senses will compensate by increasing the competence of the observational abilities of their other senses. The memorable language acquisition accomplishments of Helen Keller, who was blind and deaf from the age of nineteen months, began with her ability to achieve observational competence through the senses of touch, taste, and smell because sight and hearing, usually those most easily accessed, were not available to her. Part of the genius of her teacher, Anne Sullivan, was her recognition of touch, taste, and smell as powerful observational tools.

As language itself begins to develop, exposure to storytelling may be one of best ways to keep these observational skills sharp and growing. Unlike activities that involve multiple forms of media, storytelling calls on the observer's senses to create stories in the interior mind. No pictures are shown. The integrity and creative power of the observer's own imagination are respected. No artificial smells or tastes are incorporated, and there are no "hands on" activities. No, all of this is mental exercise in the storytelling observer's own imagination.

For the parent or teacher who says, "But I can't tell stories," reading aloud—either from books that have no illustrations or without showing the illustrations—can offer many of the same observational exercises.

The Second Dimension (strand two): Imitation of What Has Been Observed

At some point along the way, that very baby who has observed that the strange sound "bottle" is regularly made by adults when a certain set of observed circumstances occur together, and that the action which accompanies the sound (the plugging of the bottle itself into his or her waiting mouth) produces satisfaction and pleasure, will undertake a mimetic experiment. Next time hunger occurs, instead of crying, the baby tries imitating the strange sound "bottle," and, lo and behold, the bottle appears and he or she is fed! A usable working word has been added to functional vocabulary.

Very quickly, other words come rushing into use as competent observation of the circumstances that call forth these sounds defines them, and as repeated imitation tests the definitions and incorporates them into functional use.

Note that it is listening that marks out the sound of the word, and observation of surrounding activity through the *other* senses which defines its meaning. When one sense is not functional, language development not only is much more difficult, but language itself is more remotely symbolic and less immediately functional than with five functional senses.

In pedestrian terminology, the imitation step might quickly be called "talking." I have chosen not to use this word, however, because imitation involves much more than is contained in the usual definition of talking. Imitation is not a consciously studied process but one of immersion in language as it is juggled back and forth between real, living people in negotiated communication with each another.

This observation and imitation soon start to entail not only vocabulary but also syntax, style, structure, and other elements of language at a rapidly accelerating rate during the first four or five years of life. Such growth depends on being able through imitation to try out what has been observed. If the opportunity to try it out is not there, growth stops.

Enter...school! All too often the imitation step is seen as bad behavior when children start to school. It is almost as if we say: "You have talked for five years. Now it is time to stop talking and be quiet!"

If language development is to be kept flowing, there must be opportunities after entry into school to try out language orally and kinesthetically (more about this later). In fact, a good writing model will recognize talking as the basic creative language with which our children arrive at the door.

Just as storytelling helps build observational skill, it is a powerful medium for *imitation of what is observed.* As a young child growing up in an oral story culture, I well remember returning from my grandmother's house and retelling to my brother or to schoolmates the traditional stories she had told to me and my cousins. In retelling, I imitated her language in form and content and used words and structures that I myself could not have generated. I am sure that the opportunity and expectation to do this helped build my observation skills as they provided an arena to try out what was observed in my own retelling. Later we will have specific suggestions for incorporating storytelling from a child's own experiences in the creative writing process.

The Third Dimension (strand three): Beginning to Read and the Mechanics of Writing

As we examine a new strand, it is important to state again that the cable works only if the first strands remain strong while the later strands are added. So dimension three is not just "Beginning to Read and the Mechanics of Writing" but must also include strong, actively practiced *observing* and *oral imitation and experimentation.* If the first-acquired dimensions are allowed to slip, the entire language cable fails. This danger increases as we add more steps.

This third dimension is often paralleled by a child's starting to school, though not necessarily so. Some children learn to read on their own, somehow, and are reading before any formal instruction ever begins. Others learn very slowly and with great difficulty even after years of schooling. For most of us, however, learning to read and write coincides with the start of school at age five or six.

This period is one of the greatest danger points for interrupting the natural and overall flow of language development. There is often a tendency when formal education begins to see language instruction and learning as *the same as* learning to read and write. It is almost as though our test-centered education structures give no language-acquisition credit to the oral and kinesthetic language growth that already has been occurring for five or six years. It is also a time when active practice and maintenance of the first two steps often end—and are sometimes even purposely cut off.

Sometimes, as noted earlier, teachers seem to say, "OK, children, you've been talking for five years now. That's enough talking. Let's all get quiet so that we can learn to read and write!"

While it is true that reading and writing may be learned simultaneously, I am placing them in two separate strands on our language-development cable. Our reading level always outruns our writing level. Children can read much harder material than they can ever write (the same is true for adults). As we first learn reading, we are simultaneously acquiring the first mechanics of writing. Later, we will move to an entirely different level, doing what might be called *creative* writing.

Let's look at some of the other dangers that

often interfere with language development at the early reading level. When we spend all our time stressing the importance of reading, there is a strong tendency to downplay stories and oral literature. If we define "literate" as being able to read and write, we ignore thousands of years of important oral literature that carried world cultures through generations of ordered and meaningful life.

There is a parallel tendency to define the "real word" as the written word, leaving children with both their own talk and their own stories devalued. It is easy for a child so taught to think that stories are found only in books and that they are created only by professional writers. I find children today who actually think that books (and, therefore, the stories in them) are made by machines and associate no human activity with this process. Some of them cannot believe that I have written the books I show them.

Soaking in stories is very difficult when all of one's language instruction time is spent reading to and for yourself slowly, one word at a time.

Of course we want children to be readers, but when we turn reading over to them totally or prematurely, we cause two problems. The first is that we deprive them of the modeling that occurs when they are read to by adults. When children read for themselves, they skip words they do not know, and they often read as fast as they can instead of savoring and soaking in the language. When we tell stories to children and adults, we model grammar and style, introduce new words that are understood by context and oral shaping, and slow listeners down so that they can imagine, interact, and visualize. We must forever read aloud and tell stories if we want people's observational powers to remain strong and grow.

The second thing we do when we turn reading completely over to new readers is limit the literature they see to an elementary style, syntax, and vocabulary. Conversely, when we tell stories and when we read aloud, we can keep children in a growing mode with stories and literature much more complex and mature than anything they can read alone.

One more problem that occurs at this level is the likelihood that a child's own oral language growth will slow or stop. When do school children have opportunities to work on their oral language development? When do they get to practice-"talking"? The answer is that talking happens mostly when they are in free-time situations with their peers: lunch, recess, and on the school bus. In such settings where peers model for peers, language levels stagnate at best—and erode at worst—rather than being raised through real and significant oral practice and modeling.

While children are learning to read, they should be telling and retelling stories at the same time. They should be telling their own experiences and retelling in their own ways (and with their own words) what they have read and heard. "Saying it to learn how to say it" in language development is like practicing music. No one learns to be a musician simply by listening to notes!

So, to wrap up this important step, we must *continue* to build growing observational skills and oral self-expression skills, and add to these beginning reading and the first mechanics of writing.

The Fourth Dimension (strand four): Creative Writing

There is a sense in which the very term "creative writing" is odd. For most of us, writing remains a *documentation* medium rather than a *creative* one; it can be brought into meaningful play only *after* prior creative steps have been effectively exercised in our more primary, and therefore more competent, oral and kinesthetic language.

More simply put, for most of us, even into adulthood, writing is a foreign language. The best we usually do is to *translate* into it, but we rarely create within it. And what do we have inside us that can be translated? We have what has been created by our most basic language toolset—the oral and kinesthetic package we absorbed in our earliest childhood.

I am not, at this point, interested in that one rare person out of dozens, or even hundreds, who loves to write and out of whom words naturally flow. No, my real interest is in coming to understand people who simply cannot write and, because of this inability to handle the medium mislabeled "creative writing," have come to believe that they have no content, no stories, within them.

Inability to engage in creative writing no more indicates that we lack "content" than inability to speak French means that we can't speak English. No, writing is not some inscription of our oral language; it is a whole new language in and of itself. Moving into this final dimension of language development requires already braided (and strongly maintained) observational skills, oral self-expression skills, reading skills, and mechanical writing skills, to which we now add the entirely new strand of the written medium. It is working effectively at this final strand of the braid that will be our focus when we explore a new model for teaching "creative writing."

These, then, are the tools we all use in acquiring our primary language: observational skills, oral self-expression skills, reading skills (and the beginnings of mechanical writing skills), and creative writing skills. But what, exactly, is being developed through this braiding process? And what are we are finally calling "language"?

Recent literacy agendas too narrowly define language as "reading and writing," and so do many educational curricula. Now that we have seen one possible model of developmental process, let us look more deeply at the matter of language itself. Our goal is to discover the multiple dimensions of language at its fullest. We want to take advantage of this wholeness in using language as a natural creative medium, and we want to see how much of it we can capture in the slender medium of the written word.

THREE

What is Language?

One might casually say that language at its highest and purest is made of words, those symbolic representations of both concrete realities and conceptual ideas, used for human communication. A lofty definition, yes…maybe. It all depends upon what is meant by the word *communication.*

In the contemporary and highly developed worlds of sales, marketing, and management, we often see "communication" used to mean "presentation." "Presentation" refers to the movement of a picture, thought, or idea from a *presenter* to a *target audience,* or receiver. This is a script-based model, and we see it used in the theater, by television and radio broadcasters (think of the word *broad-cast* for a moment!), in the university lecture hall, the criminal courtroom, and the church pulpit. In this model, the "fourth wall" that in classical theater separates the audience from the stage may just as well be the television screen in our living room. The television talks to us and shows us things, but we can neither talk back nor influence in any way (not even to altering speed of speech) the message, information, or opinion that is being presented to us.

Presentation is a language medium that does *not* make full use of the language arsenal we have just described in this book. Presentation cannot, then, be a model that exercises our whole available language. Thus, in school, when drama and speech are studied, both can easily fall short of being "communications" fields, because they may be looked at in very scripted and one-sided ways.

To get a fuller grasp of the word "communication" and the scope of the language it uses, we must go to our Latin roots. Our English word *communication* comes from the Latin *communicare,* which also happens to be the parent word for such English words as *communicable, communion,* and *community.* All these words refer to conditions, activities, or places involving the participation of more than one person or more than "one side."

In short, "communication" is a function of relational language in all of its two-sidedness. A television broadcast can move information. But it cannot, by definition, "communicate" because the watcher or listener and the broadcaster do not simultaneously participate together in moving the pictures and ideas from one to the other, or in seeing that the broadcaster's intent matches the receiver's understanding.

With communication as our model, we are defining language as an entity larger and infinitely more complex and powerful than language viewed as a presentation tool. At the same time, we are looking at an entity that, except for vocabulary, syntactical prowess, and ability to document (we call it "writing"), can usefully be mastered by the average five-year-old.

What, then, are the multiple dimensions of this thing we call our "language"?

Five Dimensions of the Oral and Kinesthetic Language Package

In an earlier book of mine entitled *Telling Your Own Stories* (August House, 1993), there is a brief discussion of the "Five Languages of Storytelling." After an additional half-dozen years of observation and refinement, I offer a much fuller treatment of that same dimensionality as we seek to understand our primary functional language. Doing this should help us tackle another language entirely, one we call writing.

Dimension One: The Language of Movement

Let us think for a moment of a baby who is too young to be talking at all, a baby who is only a few months old and has not yet acquired even her first word. No words...does that mean no language? Of course not! At least two or three, and probably four, of the language dimensions described next already are being competently developed in the pre-word-verbal child, and the first is the language of movement.

A great deal of what the young child observes

at that first level of observational competence discussed earlier is related to touch and body movement. Soon the pre-verbal child is learning that much can be communicated with others by body movement—the language of gesture.

Using this new language, the baby may either reach out to mama or turn away from her. She may rock and sway contentedly or lash out at the whole world with flailing arms, legs, and writhing torso. Very early, we begin to acquire and use a competent language of movement and gesture that remains available to us all our lives.

Gesture is such a powerful language that it is even possible for totally deaf people to compensate by using a system of "organized gestures" or "sign language."

Still, for the hearing and non-hearing alike, it is our most *natural* gestures that provide key language tools for communication. Once, while being signed at a storytelling festival, I was told by a fine interpreter that she wanted to position herself so that the audience would see both of us at the same time. When I inquired about this, she said, "I don't want them to look away from you in order to watch me. You see, they already understand about half of the content of your stories from your *gestural language.* If I have them watching you, I can then fill in the rest."

After the event, our discussion of gestural language continued. Eventually I realized that in her work she metaphorically defines "sign language" as "gestures organized to compensate for the inability to hear." This very powerful language dimension literally enables the speechless to speak.

Gestural language even has its own volume levels. Some of us have very low "gestural volume" as a matter of overall kinesthetic language. That is, we tend to communicate with very little body language. If our gestural volume is low, our hands tend to stay near a resting position, we do not use pronounced facial expressions, and we do not move about much when we are communicating. Others of us are "high volume" gestural communicators. We use our hands and arms wildly, our faces are like rubber, and our whole bodies are in motion all the time.

Some of these gestural volume differences may be personal habit, and some may be cultural. Two different friends of mine have reported on extensive work as storyteller and photographer among native peoples in the farthest northern parts of Alaska. My storyteller friend reported that, upon first arrival, she visited the school and told stories to the schoolchildren there. Her initial reaction to their reception was almost one of despair. "They just sat there and didn't move at all... I was totally convinced that they didn't get what I was talking about, and I really didn't want to go back again."

It was a great surprise to her when the report came that the children had loved the storytelling and wanted her to return and tell again as soon as possible. "How can this be?" she asked a new acquaintance who taught at this same school.

The answer that came from the teacher was the same answer that came from my photographer friend, himself a northern Alaska native. "Do two things and you will understand. When you go to school tomorrow to tell stories, look only at their *faces* and, at the same time, remember how people in this climate have dressed for as long as there has been human habitation here!"

The next day the storyteller did just that and realized that the entire range of gestural language was present within the faces of her listeners. Traditionally, the rest of these people's bodies had been heavily covered up by clothing, so the face was the only available "gestural instrument" that developed as a physical communication tool.

As we consider this anecdote, we might also think of those cultures whose people we caricature as "talking with their hands." We realize that these are warm-climate cultures. Could it be that our entire body develops as a communication instrument to the extent that it is available (visible) to be put to such use? I make no defensible scientific assertions because there is not documentation to do so. But I do raise the question based on our common anecdotal observations.

Even though all of us have our own basic gestural volumes, we each make adjustments in the same way and for the same reasons that we adjust the volume level of our voices. When we are "talking" with only one person or a small group, our gestural volume remains at its lowest normal level. That is all we need when communicating one-on-one. As the group of people to whom we are talking grows larger, more gestural volume is required. For example, we may remain seated to tell a story or make a presentation to a dozen people. When the number grows to thirty, suddenly we need to stand up. As the number in the audience grows larger and larger, we move around more and more and become more and more physical.

Gestural volume also changes with emotional levels, just as does vocal volume. When we are calm, our gestures are small and limited. As we grow more excited, either positively or negatively, our gestures become larger and the physical dimension of our communicating becomes much "louder."

Remember the interpreter for the deaf who gave me my first lesson in understanding the real functional power of gesture? After the storytelling festival at which she had signed for me, we watched a group of deaf listeners "talking" in American Sign Language about the performance they had just heard. *"Look* at how *loudly* they are talking!" she said. "When I see them talking that loudly, I know they have had a good time!" Sure enough, it was clear to the eyes of anyone who watched that they did, indeed, "speak" with gestural *loudness.*

All this is just to say that the gestural dimension of our primary language is a large and usable dimension, and that we absorb gestural competence without even realizing it from the language modeling of the family, tribe, or culture we grow up in. It is also true that we can learn to enhance our use of gestural language once we understand its potential power.

Dimension Two: The Language of Sound

The second dimension of our primary oral and kinesthetic language is the *language of sound.* By this we do not mean orally spoken words, but rather non-word sound itself.

The language of sound includes the sound shaping we use to give spoken words their gradations and even reversals of meaning. It also includes such sound dynamics as pitch, speed of speech, timbre, timing, and pauses.

From birth, pre-word children are already absorbing and learning to use the language of sound. They can communicate in a sound language that ranges from the contented gurgling of happiness and satisfaction to the kind of screaming that is so loud their voices crack and the sound won't even come out any more.

Let us look at some dynamics of this language dimension.

First, let us consider sound shaping of known words. On the printed page a particular word looks the same to the reader's eye no matter what its minute gradations of meaning might happen to be. Suppose we had a cadre of a dozen or so normal thirteen-year-olds. Let us give each of them a slip of paper with a word written on it. We will give each the same word and ask then if, using sound, he or she can speak it aloud, giving it a different meaning from those offered by other students. For this simple test, let us give them the word *mother*.

We quickly realize that even though the word *mother* looks the same on the printed page no matter what it means, all of the dozen thirteen-year-olds can make it move through a wide range of meanings. With their use of the language of sound, the word *mother* can in one moment be a term of endearment and in the next a label of utter disgust; it can in one instance be a plea for help and in the next an expletive of excessively profane proportions—all this through the language of sound.

One of the most powerful oral and kinesthetic language skills is what comedians, actors, and effective speakers often call "timing." Timing is built mostly of sound (with a little help from gesture).

One easy example. The speaker or storyteller starts a sentence, then pauses for a moment just before saying aloud the final word. During that pregnant pause, all the listeners are, without even realizing it, finishing the sentence in their own minds. Then, the speaker finishes the sentence he or she started.

If listeners hear the sentence end in exactly the same way (and even with the same word) that they guessed, they feel brilliant and perceptive and believe the speaker to be brilliant and perceptive as well. But if the speaker finishes the sentence in an entirely different way and totally fools the listeners, the result is, if possible, even better! Now listeners are thinking, "I never would have thought of that," and at the same time are laughing appreciatively and believing the speaker to be truly brilliant.

It may even be that poetry could be metaphorically defined as "the attempt to effect timing on the printed page." In poetic writing the physical layout of the lines themselves adds rhythm and pauses that might have been missing if the same words were simply laid out as margin-to-margin prose on the printed page.

The language of sound includes the language of pitch. The natural pitch of an individual's voice is part of that person's own personal language of sound. Pitch can be changed and worked with, no matter what the normal pitch of one's voice. Therefore, pitch may be used to communicate mood and feeling, to imitate another person's voice, or even to imitate animals or other sounds from the natural world. The language of sound is used when we talk fast as well as when we speak slowly and with great deliberateness.

The language of sound, that second tool in our natural oral and kinesthetic language package, is so usably powerful that the person who masters its intricacies has as many subtleties to work with in communicating spoken words as does the skilled vocal musician in interpreting songs.

Dimension Three: The Language of Attitude and Emotion

I initially learned about the language of attitude and emotion at the storytelling festival where I was taught by the earlier mentioned interpreter for the deaf.

In my first conversation with this American Sign Language specialist (when she had said she wanted her section of the audience to look at me while she signed), she went on to add another language dimension that I had not thought of before.

"Besides gesture," (I paraphrase her) "they will understand an additional portion of your story by observing your *attitudinal* language."

When I asked, "What is attitudinal language?" the answer was, "Oh...you must not have had a teenager at home for awhile!" With that, I understood what she meant.

The *language of attitude and emotion* is that package of clues we give, both kinesthetically and orally, revealing how we feel about what we are saying. It reflects our normal inability to hide feelings, beliefs, and emotions.

To illustrate this, when talking with students, I often ask a simple question: "Did any of you ever have a teacher whom everyone knew hated teaching and disliked being around kids?" Almost always they shake their heads affirmatively, having just visualized a personal example.

Then I ask them: "Did that teacher actually tell you with words that he or she hated being a teacher and, in fact, did not like spending each day with you?" The unanimous head shake now changes to the negative. "No," I remember one little boy saying, "you can just see it and hear it in their voice…you can just *feel* it!"

The language of attitude and emotion is a powerful part of our total communication package. In the criminal courtroom, the jury watches and listens carefully, trying to determine the believability of what is being communicated by the attitude and emotion of the witness. It is this dimension of language that we rely on to assess our feeling of the truthfulness or falsity of what we are being told.

The language of attitude and emotion helps us decide whether people like us or not, whether they enjoy being with us, whether they believe in what they are doing or saying, and whether they are totally present or are just physically going through the motions.

In addition, teachers are familiar with the skillful use of this language dimension by students to bend events (or facts) to fit their own opinions. Nothing is quite as frustrating to a teacher than to watch and listen to a student *literally* carry out instructions while attitudinally and emotionally doing the very opposite of what is being asked for. "Do you understand the assignment?" the teacher asks. All heads, faces, and voices say, "Yes!" Yet, tomorrow, these same students will swear that it was not *clearly* stated.

While these anecdotal illustrations attest to the fact that there is such a thing as attitudinal language, is it possible to describe this language dimension more precisely? Is not attitudinal language just another part of what we demonstrate gesturally rather than a different dimension?

This answer is partially yes. We can sometimes "see" attitude clearly communicated gesturally. For example, if we look out a second story window and observe two people talking in the park across the street, we can "see" the attitude each has toward the other. This is not, however, the whole story. We can also "hear" attitude in a telephone conversation with another person we cannot even see. Did you ever talk with a telemarketer who actually "sounded" as if he or she loved that job?

Attitudinal language cannot be defined empirically, but failing to note and make use of it as a communication (and an observational) tool ignores a key help we have as communicators.

So far we have talked about three dimensions of our usable primary language: the gestural language of movement, the non-word language of sound itself, and the difficult-to-define language of attitude and emotion. We have not yet, however, made reference to the direct use of words. Nor shall we now, for there is still another important language dimension to consider before moving to the oral word.

Dimension Four: The Language of Listener Molding

Several years ago I was spending a week at a middle school in South Carolina. It was one of those schools where they do not let the students into the building until after the first bell rings. Even though they were early for school, students arrived a good while before they knew they could go in. It was easy to see why. They had come to visit with one another.

One day I asked them, "What do you do when you get here early in the morning before they will let you into the school building?"

I already knew their answer. "We talk!" they said, almost proudly.

"What do you do when you are the first one to get here?" I continued.

"We wait for somebody to talk to," was the answer.

"Why don't you just go ahead and start talking without waiting for anyone else to come?" I pushed them. "You'd get a head start on all the others if you went ahead and started talking before they got here!"

Everyone laughed, then one student spoke for all of them. "Silly...you can't talk without somebody to talk to!"

Did you ever stop to realize that we rarely "just talk" (except for those of us who mutter to ourselves); we usually talk *to* or *with* someone else, to or with another person. It is, in fact, very difficult to talk out loud with no one to talk to. If I said to you, "Go into that empty room and talk out loud for one hour about the trip you just came back from," could you do it? Yet we could go on for hours about the same trip in a bar or at a party where there were other people listening to us.

Why is this? In Isak Dinesen's book *Out of Africa,* the narrator tells us that everyone looks forward to when Denis Finch-Hatton comes, for when Denis comes, there are stories. Does Denis tell stories? No, the narrator informs us that the stories come out of people when Denis comes because Denis is *such a good listener*.

The faces that are looking at us as we talk draw stories out from us. The face is like a magnet pulling at the teller and saying with gestural language: "Tell me more . . . Explain that a bit . . . Describe the scene . . . What happened after that? . . . I am interested in you and in your story."

Not only is the listening face pulling the story from us, but it is our first helpful editor in the story assembly process. When the listening face looks puzzled, we expand with illustrative details. When the face smiles or looks happy or even laughs, it is the same as saying, "I see it!" and we know that that part of our story is clear and adequate. When the listening face gives us a "that's dumb" or a "no way" response, we begin editing that part out of the story or molding it into something else.

A fully usable dimension of our language is

the knowledge that the listener effectively molds the story being listened to. We watch and change, watch and change, over against the look on our listener's face.

Try this experiment, but don't try it on those you need to live with! The next time someone comes quickly toward you and wants to tell something that is exciting to him or her, look blank and pretend that you simply don't get it at all. Watch the teller back the story up and try to start it all over again. You still don't get it. The teller starts over again but will not be able to go forward until you somehow affirm your understanding and acceptance of what you are being told. In communication we are dependent on the molding feedback of our listeners to help us shape the content and form of the story we are telling or the message we are giving.

That this is true is further illustrated by the way in which we pretend instant understanding when we want to get rid of someone we don't want to spend a lot of time in conversation with. When the teacher gives the homework assignment, one of the reasons that the entire seventh-grade class nods with understanding and pretends to have taken it all in with no questions at all is to move the teacher on and get him or her to stop talking about this homework stuff any longer. When we see someone coming along the sidewalk whom we'd rather avoid, we simply pretend to grasp exactly what he or she says immediately.

That response of affirmation usually gets people on their way and out of ours.

This is a helpful live language dimension that the writer working with words on paper does not have. The writer has no listener's face offering helpful questions or affirmations in the very process of putting the story together. The writer is a lone worker trying to guess and guess and guess at what is clear and when enough is enough or not enough. The oral and kinesthetic communicator has as many helpers as he or she has listeners. Each listening face lifts, pulls, helps us do a better and clearer job with our story.

Learning to use this dimension, learning to read and respond to the help offered by the faces of the molding listeners, learning to make use of the free energy offered to us by our audience, takes us a long way in effective communication. The baby begins to learn this skill quickly and tailors laughter and tears to the parents' molding responses. However, when we move into scripted educational and presentation processes, this is a skill that is dangerously easy to lose.

All too often the main evaluative question in a script-based event is, "Did I say all the words?" In the world of communication, the event is negotiated with the faces of the listeners, always asking, "Are they getting it?" and continually remodeling the story until that clarity is affirmed.

Dimension Five: Orally Spoken Words

After all this, we come to the final dimension of our naturally absorbed oral and kinesthetic language: the use of words spoken orally.

A common assumption about language is that it is *either* oral or written. Our look at these five dimensions shows us that such a distinction is far too simplistic. There is in reality no such thing as language that is merely oral. The word-spoken-orally is only a part of a larger oral and kinesthetic package.

Perhaps the oral dimension represents the content *center* of our oral and kinesthetic language, and perhaps the other dimensions we have discussed are clarifiers, enhancers, and enablers of clear meaning. Still, transcription into writing of words spoken orally carries with it only a part of the wholeness of the story being told.

An important task we will come to later as we enter the writing process is our realization that, in writing, we must write much more than would ever have been spoken in order to tell exactly the same story. When we move into writing, we must learn to compensate for losing the use of movement, sound, attitude, and feedback by using *more words*. However, this will come later.

So, these are our five dimensions and dynamics of that primary oral and kinesthetic language package we have called "our first language." Now that we have surveyed this primary language, let us consider it beside the acquisition skills we sketched out earlier to see how they all fit together.

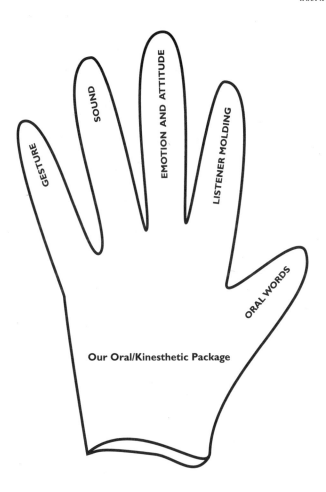

GESTURE

SOUND

EMOTION AND ATTITUDE

LISTENER MOLDING

ORAL WORDS

Our Oral/Kinesthetic Package

FOUR

Soaking Up Our Primary Language

Looking back at the various features of primary language as we have defined them, we see that each of the earlier strands of acquisition applies directly to other dimensions. For example, it is *observational competence* that enables the developing child to incorporate particular *gestural language* usages into the vocabulary of movement. This same competence at observation leads to the acquisition and continuing growth of the languages of *sound* and *attitude.*

But the most important thing to note about these connections is that unless oral and kinesthetic language is *modeled,* neither the acquisition competencies nor the language dimensions themselves have any chance of being acquired. Primary oral and kinesthetic language is not taught. None of us has any objective awareness or memory of being "taught" to talk, gesture, or use emotion in communication. Our primary language is simply absorbed—"soaked up" from the pool of language that we experience as young children. The very presence of regional accents, brogues, and dialects in speech is clear evidence of this reality. The soaking, however, goes far beyond accent. In the earlier stages of language development, we acquire *only* what is modeled for us. Our vocabulary, grammar, syntax, structure, and other language dimensions are direct reflections of the language in which we soak until the time when we are able consciously to effect change and growth in our primary language as "adults."

Let us look at a pair of models illustrating what this may mean in the child's language development. In earlier times when humans lived in tribes or extended families, prior to computers, television and day-care, preschool children stayed at home and played while the adults who were with them talked and went about their own business. Those talking adults may have included extended family members such as grandparents, aunts, and uncles as well as neighbors and other family friends. Adult language was the background "noise" for child's play. While the children were tending to their own play agenda, they were in an arena where they could observe adults in language interaction with one another. Gradually, youngsters absorbed what they saw and heard.

Add to this play environment a world of oral storytelling and orally preserved and transmitted literature and we are in a world in which language is highly modeled and may naturally grow onward through observational skill to all five of the dimensions we have just laid out.

Now, move time forward toward the present. What happens when the young child is removed from a play environment in which adult conversation is the background to a play environment in a day-care setting where the only surrounding sounds are peers of the same age and language level? What model is there now to absorb?

What happens when, instead of a world of orally carried stories in one's own family or community, there is a television set running in the background filled with commercial jingles (at best) and talk-back interview shows (at worst) as the child's language model? What kinds of language skills and usages are modeled by cartoon shows and by the majority of videos marketed for "younger children"?

What happens when we are all computerized and the child is linked visually to a highly defined computer screen but is hearing and seeing almost no living, interactive language as practiced by real humans whom he knows, loves, and respects?

If adequate modeling for primary language has not occurred, then *that* may be our first task in teaching the language arts and building the foundation towards later growth in writing. In other words, if we receive children at an entry level in school (or much later) whose language has been television-taught, then we must spend whatever time and energy it takes to outmodel television.

Many new readers love to read, but, whenever we turn reading completely over to an elementary child, what happens to language modeling? When children do all their own reading, what they can manage never rises above their own personal competence level. They tend to skip over the words they do not know and often read as fast as possible to finish assignments. In addition, when reading for themselves, they never hear the sounds of the less familiar words in order to know how to use them in their own language. When one of my own children was once building a model car, he figured out what the kit's decals were for. But reading the instructions only for himself and never having had that word modeled for his observation, he came proudly displaying and telling all about the "diesels" he had now applied to his finished car.

For the sake of good language modeling, we must continue to read aloud, with interpretation and animation, to learners of all ages, not what they could read very well for themselves, but literature just above the level of their own competent reading. In this way we push the maintenance and growth of observational skills and build the model for language to "grow into."

When I was in the third grade, I had a new teacher who had never taught third grade before. Her name was Miss Metcalf, and we loved her because she was not old like we thought all our teachers had to be.

Since it was Miss Metcalf's first year in teaching, there were lots of things she did not know about eight-year-old children. One was that we were not old enough to be able to understand *Little Women* and *Silas Marner*. Every day after eating lunch in the school cafeteria, we returned to our third-grade classroom and listened for twenty to thirty minutes while Miss Metcalf read aloud to us, with great animation and interpretation (and sometimes vocabulary clarification) *Little Women* for the first half of the year and *Silas Marner* for the second half.

Now, since we were only eight years old, there were a lot of things we also did not know about ourselves. One of them was that we were not supposed to be old enough to understand *Little Women* and *Silas Marner*. Since we didn't know any better, we absolutely loved it! I still see to this very day scenes in my head from both of those wonderful books that were read aloud to us.

No, we could never have read them ourselves. We were still studying some third-grade version of *Dick and Jane*, but, when Miss Metcalf read, not only did we see all the pictures in our own heads, we had language patterned and modeled for us, from style and grammar to vocabulary and idiom. Nothing could have lifted us more effectively than the simple act of that daily thirty-minute model.

You may very well say, "I do not believe that children today could do that." If so, then my point is made, and the need is greater still. I, too, doubt that most children today could do what we did. Instead of soaking in the adult language of an orally competent society, today's youngters may be woefully lacking in the skills associated with primary language development.

It seems an anomaly that people who were less formally educated could have possessed greater language skills than the Head-Started children of today, but this is seen over and over again when we compare vocabularies in the literature of the first half of our century and current publications for the same age or grade levels in our schools. I have even had pointed out to me examples of literature from third- or fourth-grade readers printed fifty years ago that now can be found in literature texts for middle or junior high school students.

As a child I would visit at my Uncle Frank's house and listen to him and Silas Jolly exchange stories on the porch. Silas was a simple and probably very slimly schooled rural neighbor, yet his language was spectacular. I still recall Uncle Frank ending a story with the statement, "And that's the truth!" To this ending Silas laughed and replied, "Yes sir, boys, that certainly was a splendid caricature of prevarication, all right!" I had to go home and ask my daddy what Silas, the unschooled talker, was talking about.

When we go back to times when life was more tribal and less electronic, when people lived as extended families and extended neighborhoods, when children played with adult conversations as the backdrop, we often find more highly developed language skills in younger children than we find at the same age levels today. In such settings, strong background language was unconsciously soaked up by the growing child and used as a model for his or her own accent, pronunciation, vocabulary, and syntax.

As a child, I grew up spending long weekends "visiting" at the homes of grandparents and various other nearby relatives. There was no television to watch and no mall to go to for shopping or eating out. My brother and my cousins and I played in the yard while all of the adults sat on the porch and talked the afternoon away. Yes, we were eavesdropping on the content of the stories and anecdotes they were sharing and the adventures they were reliving with one another. More importantly, though, we were soaking in an environment of good adult language that nourished our own language growth. As we heard words that were new to us, we gradually gathered from context and other surrounding evidence their meanings without ever being told. As we heard various syntax and speech patterns, they became our own syntax and speech patterns. Language modeled is language learned.

Once more let us think briefly about the language environment in which today's child may grow up. It may be a passive child-care environment where the overwhelming bulk of language comes from same-age peers with no background music of adult conversation. At home, it may be the world of television with the language of cartoons and talk shows as models. In either case, we should not be surprised at the lack of functional oral language in our school-age children; and if they spend a large part of their time looking at computer screens, they may get *no* oral model at all to help them move beyond immature language.

Let us restate the modeling agenda. It can be possible that with acquired observational competence we may soak up gestural, sound, attitudinal, oral, and feedback dynamics of language so that we may then try them out until they become part of our language arsenal. But without positive modeling, our language level at best slows and at worst starts to erode.

Before we leave this area, let us look at a closing metaphor as we think not about the fact of language development, but rather about its importance.

The metaphor is a computer. Often I will throw out to people an unfinished sentence: "When you have a computer, you have the *hardware*, which is the computer itself, but you also have to have_____." The crowd will in unison answer "software." Of course they have finished the sentence correctly.

Then I ask, "Do you need anything else besides hardware and software to work a computer program?" I am usually met with blank stares or flat answers of "no." Then I remind them that the way in which Bill Gates became the richest person in America was by figuring out that computer hardware could not run computer software without some sort of "language" to run on. We sometimes call such language the "operating system." The Microsoft fortune was not made by creating software application programs, but by creating the very language itself that enables everything else to work.

The earliest version of this operative language was MS-DOS, short for the "Microsoft Disk Operating System." Did the operating system language stay at that level? No, in order to run more and more complex software on more and more powerful computers, the language grew through multiple upgrades of MS-DOS, then on to WINDOWS, WINDOWS 95, WINDOWS 98, and surely this is not the end.

The frightening thing about this metaphor is that, when we look at its human counterpart, we realize it is language itself that enables us to run the software programs that in school we call courses (history, mathematics, literature, and sciences). Without our operative human language, the application programs cannot run, nor can effective life skills be practiced.

The second frightening thing to realize is that our own parents and grandparents may have started school having already soaked up an oral and kinesthetic language equivalent to WINDOWS 98, while the children of today, whom we are pushing harder and harder in terms of academic applications, are coming to school with the personal operative language equivalent of MS-DOS 1.0!

Long before we can even begin to talk about writing, we must look seriously at the wholeness of this language-development process, look seriously at where our children are in terms of their primary oral and kinesthetic competence, and work long and hard to nourish those practices that keep that most basic functional language not only alive but positively growing for life.

In short, we must tell more stories and tell more stories and tell more stories and then, read and read and read, aloud, forever.

FIVE

Let's Begin to Think About Writing

Using Story as a Model for Creative Writing

What is a story, anyway, and how have we made the very idea of writing a story so hard? As we move toward the development of a writing model, one thing we must do is to identify stumbling blocks that, for various reasons and from various sources, have come to make writing even harder than it should be for us. If we can identify and then simply remove some of these stumbling blocks, then we will have moved a long way toward creative writing without actively adding any new knowledge at all. Let us take a look at a major stumbling block and some ways to remove it from blocking us.

From the very beginnings of working with reading and writing in school, we do something with children that makes writing a story very difficult later on. It is what I might call, for lack of a better term, "plot obsession."

Either think back to the time when you were learning to read, or observe younger children in the classroom as they are learning to read today. Now, more than their work at reading, note the questions we ask them about what they are reading (or the questions we were asked) to check on comprehension.

To illustrate, let me share a trick I often use with young readers. I have tried this dozens of times with young readers, and the result has always been the same. When with a group of young readers, I first ask the question, "Can you read?" The answer is a unanimous "yes." My next question is, "Does your teacher ever ask you to read, and then ask questions about what you have just read?" Again, the answer is "yes."

Now the real question comes into play. "Now, children, think with me. Does your teacher ever say, 'Read this story and then tell me what _____.'" As soon as I pause, the children unanimously answer, "Tell me what *happened*." "So," I continue, "the teacher asks you to read the story and then tell what happened?

"Does the teacher ever say, 'Read the story and then tell me what the grandmother's house looked like?'" The heads shake "no." I continue, "Does the teacher ever say, 'Read the story and then tell me what you think Big George's dog smelled like when it got wet?'" Again the heads shake "no."

"Happened" is a plot word. In fact, by the time children have moved along in reading for another grade or two, we are actually asking, "Read the story and tell me the plot...read the story and outline the plot…read the story and summarize the plot…read the story and analyze the plot in terms of…" All the way to graduate school one may study literature and never be asked to look at anything except the plot.

Some years ago a fellow figured this dynamic out and made a fortune in the process. When he realized that the only questions we are likely to be asked about literature are plot questions, a young man named Cliff started to publish what we all today know as *Cliffs Notes*, those plot summaries that have pulled countless students out of the mire of procrastination at exam time.

When we are asked only about plot, over and over again, a little formula about what stories are made of is being burned into our brains. The formula begins: "Story…tell me the plot…story… plot…story…plot…story…*equals* plot!" Later on, when it is time to write a story, that same brain starts talking to us, saying, "So, you have to write a story…then what you must need is a plot!" Then there is panic because we do not have a plot, and we can sit for hours and accomplish nothing except a growing awareness of our own ineptitude and a convincing reaffirmation of our lack of creativity.

Let us take a fuller look at what stories are made of and see whether we can break this problem and find a better beginning place.

First of all, let's think about stories we have heard or read and have never forgotten. When you think of your favorite story, do you recall the words it was made of, or do you see the story in your own visual imagination? Again and again, when I ask this question after I have told a story, people unanimously reply, "I see it!"

Have you ever been reading a book that was so riveting that you could not put it down to do anything else? At that captivating moment, were you actually reading *words*, or were you really *watching* the story as it unfolded in your visual imagination? Again, when I ask this question, people unanimously reply, "I was watching it!" This is the kind of reading about which we later say, "The book was better than the movie" because we already made our own movie as we read along.

This brings us to our most basic assertion about what story is. When story works, it is a *visually based,* not a *word-based* entity. In other words, as listeners, when a story really works for us, we are not listening, we are watching. As readers, when a story really works for us, we are not reading, we are watching.

All this is to say that at its most basic level, story is not word, it is picture. Word just happens to be the medium in which the writer processes, develops, and fixes the pictures for others to be able to look at them.

What this means for writers is: no picture, no story! Put another way, a story is a picture I have in my head that I would like for you to have in your head. As a writer, if I do not go through the mental pre-writing process of picture development, I am frozen and can sit for hours, yea days, without any production ever occurring.

Let's think about this dilemma further in relation to what I earlier called "plot obsession." Which parts of a story can be visualized by us as listeners and as readers? Can you, without even closing your eyes, "see" a house that you remember living in when you were a child? Can we visualize places when we are not even there? Of course we can. We not only can "see" a place that is well described, we can actually hear sounds, smell smells, taste and touch. (It is important to note in passing that, while we are using the term "visualize," we are actually referring to an internal mental projection that at times may include more, perhaps even all, of our senses. This will be a point of some importance as we later move into writing.)

Can we see people we have never met? Of course we can. If you ever knew her, can you still "see" your grandmother even if she has been dead for many years? In good storytelling as in good writing, when characters are well described we not only come to see them, we know their personalities, their feelings, their needs and desires, and their hurts and pains.

Now comes the trick question. Can we see a plot? What? You don't even understand the question? While place and person are concrete, plot is really an abstraction. We devise it *after* we have come, by listening or by reading, to see the places and the people who populate them. To visualize plot without seeing people and place is an activity far beyond the capability of most writers of any age and especially beyond the capacity of the young writer.

How do we get from here into writing? Let us lay out a course of action that takes into account how our language is acquired and how it works. We will attend to the primary language in which our creative thinking is done, the losses of that primary language that have been brought about by the electronic media, and the visual nature of story. Our goal is to unlock frozen young writers, show their capacities, and build in them excitement for writing itself.

PART TWO

Developing a Workable Model for Writing

SIX

Building (and Rebuilding) Skills

A great deal of modeling is necessary to rebuild mental "picturing" as an active and competent language skill. This is an essential beginning place since the ability to visualize in pre-writing is germane to positing initial ideas, to building place and person, and to recognizing plot possibilities later on. No mental picture means no story.

We do this simply by telling and reading a lot of stories. As we tell and read, we begin to ask a new set of questions that are not about plot. Instead, all our initial questions should be about places and people.

If you are uncomfortable telling stories, or if you are using this process to work on your own personal writing, here is a methodology for strengthening visualization and reading skills. First, choose a short story by one of your favorite authors or from the age-keyed bibliography in the back of this book. Let's say that, for example, you are teaching sixth graders and that you have chosen, from my own collection *Listening for the Crack of Dawn* (August House, 1990), the story entitled, "L S / M F T."

Do not begin to read the story quickly! Whether you are reading to yourself or reading aloud to others, go slowly. In fact, even if you are reading to yourself, you might want to read aloud in order to slow down.

Read aloud, to the class or to yourself, only the first sentence: "When I got to the sixth grade, we moved to town."

Stop and ask this question: "What can we *see* from this one sentence?" At first it may take some discussion and thoughtful mental digging. "How old is the narrator as we begin to visualize? Where are we? Can we tell, from this one sentence, anything about the time period? Can we say yet who is present in the story? Would looking at information about the author or publication data help answer any of these questions? Are there any sounds, tastes, smells, and textures?"

These are the kinds of issues I want to raise—not questions about plot but about places, times, and people. It is very important to note that recognition of negative answers and missing information is also helpful in this process. Marking what we don't yet know helps us begin to see what we are still actively looking for.

If we had chosen my story in the same collection entitled "Dr. York, Miss Winnie, and the Typhoid Shot," we would find it opening with the following sentence: "Dr. York drove a Studebaker." What questions would have to be answered before a group of today's sixth-grade students could "see" a Studebaker? What would they be able to tell about "Dr. York" simply from thinking about his name? (For example, what might his profession be? Where might he or his ancestors have come from?)

We are often, in school, pushed and pushed to read more and more quickly. When we read quickly from the very start of the story, it is often difficult to "see" (and also to smell, taste, hear, and touch) the places and the people forming the container that holds the happenings we call "plot." We may be able to skim place and person description and get as quickly as possible to plot if we are speed-reading. But in the short run, such speed robs our reading of its vitality and life, and in the long run, we do not remember much of what we read because we have no visual container in our mind for carrying the plot.

Visualizing place and person can be the keys both to meaningful understanding and meaningful remembering. Later on we will see that the ability to visualize place and person well are among the most important keys to competent writing.

To push this process further, let us back up to the beginning of the "L S / M F T" story and see what happens if we move through a few more sentences and use them to "look around" as we ease into the story.

Read aloud slowly: "Daddy borrowed Uncle Floyd's pick-up truck and we hauled load after load from the house on Richland Creek for nearly three miles all the way to the other side of Sulpher Springs." Ask all the visualization questions again, adding any others that the listeners may now be challenged to think of themselves. For example, "How big a place do you think Sulpher Springs is from this opening statement?" "When do you think the events in this story took place?"

Suddenly a student asks, "What time period is this supposed to be, anyway?" As students begin to ask such questions of their own, we can almost see the pictures forming inside their heads. We are not asking at all about *happening* or *meaning* or *interpretation*. We are simply asking: "What can you see?"

Here follows the first page of that same story. Experiment with it yourself to see what happens if you try to look at it one sentence at a time.

"L S / M F T"

When I got to the sixth grade, we moved to town. Daddy borrowed Uncle Floyd's pick-up truck and we hauled load after load from the house on Richland Creek for nearly three miles all the way to the other side of Sulpher Springs. The new house was up in town, on a well-populated street named "East Street."

East Street ran downhill toward the center of town, finally crossing "Old Main" and ending at Railroad Street. The section where we lived was well over a mile from Main Street and near the top of the biggest downhill slope on the street's entire run into town.

From near our house, East Street sloped down and continued to slope down, almost straight, for over half a mile. Then it flattened out, made a ninety-degree turn to the right, and dropped downhill again.

The most wonderful thing about living on East Street, for a sixth-grade boy, was that no girls lived there. This fact of gender was not just true when our family lived there; it had always been true. For generations, as long as anyone could remember, no girls had ever been born into any families living on East Street hill.

People would say, "If you want to have a girl, you might as well move out of there. It'll never happen. But if you want to have a boy, just go buy you a house over on East Street—or at least spend the night over there once in a while. There's something in the water."

It was an obvious advantage to male sixth graders to live in an atmosphere totally devoid of female opinions, advice, or interference.

From *Listening for the Crack of Dawn* (August House, 1990)

By the time we can really see *place* (including the time frame) and *people* clearly and concretely, we can easily speed up our reading. Now *plot* is both understood and carried in memory by the visual awareness of place and person in the listener's and reader's mind.

No matter what grade level I am teaching, I never want to stop modeling such reading and listening. In an electronic age when pictures are so easily accessed mechanically without engaging one's own imagination, such exercise is much more important to language building than it was in pre-television days.

Before going on to the next stage as we move toward writing, let us add a word about regularly taking time to have children read aloud *no matter how old they get*. We almost always have children read aloud in the earliest grades when they are first learning. Very soon, though, there is a push for silent reading. This often comes with the unspoken, or spoken, assumption that speed is our main reading goal. I can still hear Mrs. Ledbetter, my own first-grade teacher, saying, "Now, boys and girls, if you say the words out loud when you read, you won't be able to read fast! Read quietly...to yourselves!"

The problem with such an approach is that it misses by a wide mark one of the most important patterning tools we can use in language growth. Having the teacher read aloud to students is an excellent tool for modeling vocabulary, syntax, and even the whole of grammar. However, having the teacher read aloud when all the students then read silently (and only to themselves) is like having a swimming teacher demonstrate strokes, then keep students from entering the water to try swimming for themselves. It is like a music teacher who plays music and only has the class listen.

Modeled language becomes useful only as it is tried out. The newly introduced word, as listened to, does not enter the vocabulary in the same way that the new word *spoken* and *used* does. The same thing is true of grammar, structure, and syntax. Our language structure grows when we speak with our own voice sentences and patterns *that we would neither write nor orally generate on our own.*

Let us return to the music metaphor. As beginning music students, we are not expected to write our own music and then play it. No, first of all (and even much later), we practice playing music written by someone else, an accomplished composer. After playing that music for a long time, we have absorbed pattern and structure enough so that we may now begin to rearrange, improvise, augment, and perhaps compose our own music. However, serious musicians never pretend that they can stop practicing the music of others and rely solely on their own musical "language." Even Mozart kept playing the music of Handel!

When we have students read aloud, we are engaging them in the same sort of learning-through-patterning activity. They are, in fact, walking paths of good language until they walk them naturally. In reading aloud, we are "forced" to speak aloud, with our own voices, words that we would not ourselves include in our own self-chosen speech. When reading aloud, we are forced to say out loud those unfamiliar words we would instantly skip over if we were reading only to ourselves. When called on to read aloud, we are forced to slow down to feel and hear each word take its place in the whole, and to listen to the balanced timing and structure of the language itself apart from the content carried by those same words. Engage learners in enough of this patterning, and proper grammatical usages will be so ingrained that they come out regularly in chosen speech.

Many of us grew up in an era when the memorization and recitation of poetry was a normal part of our language arts education. That practice has today largely been abandoned when teachers say, "I don't see the point of memorization," or "We just don't have time for that." If we return to our music metaphor, however, that objection is a bit like saying, "We don't have time to look at the perfected work of the ages...just hit the keys and play anything you want to!"

Memorizing poetry is not about memorization any more than memorizing multiplication tables is about memorization, per se. No, memorization of poetry is purely and simply about language patterning.

When, in the eighth grade in Mr. Roy Haupt's

class, I learned "L'envoi," "The Deacon's Master-piece," "Because I Could Not Stop for Death," "The Minuet," and many other poems I treasure to this day, what I was really doing was absorbing the language, the syntax, the vocabulary, and the overall language structures of Rudyard Kipling, Oliver Wendell Holmes, Emily Dickinson, Mary Mapes Dodge, and many others. The effect was that later, in my own language usage, those patterns would emerge more as my own norm than what I heard modeled around me on the school bus or on the playground.

A good friend who is a preschool teacher has for several years now been introducing her four-year-olds to poetry. In the first place, she has discovered that the children love it. They love the rhythms and rhymes of the language of poetry. They are also experiencing firsthand a growth of language that feels like the acquisition of pure power—and it is! Their own use of language is daily growing and growing as a result of this patterning. Their favorite public activity has also become "performing" poetry for adults.

Recently I was in a school residency and observed a wonderful fourth-grade teacher playing a vocabulary game with her students. In a basket she had the letter tiles from a Scrabble game. In her hand she had one of a pair of dice. As she worked around the group, a student would first draw a letter from the basket and then throw the die. The player had to come up with a word that started with the drawn letter and had the same number of syllables as the number rolled on the die. Students ended their turns by making sentences with the words they came up with. There seemed to be no grading going on. Rather it was just "exercising."

As I watched, a girl reached into the basket and pulled out the letter "v." Then she rolled the die and three dots came up. Almost immediately her three-syllable word came out: "vacuous." While I was still in thought, trying to come up with a sentence I would make with this word, she came out with her sentence. "In the teachers' lounge, our teachers often engage in vacuous prattle."

When the game was all over, I had to ask her. "How did you think up that sentence?" She gave that best of all possible answers, the one that always indicates that learning has been fully internalized: "I don't know...it just came out." Then she added, "I must have heard something like that somewhere...I guess in a story or in a poem." I could not keep from thinking about what kind of word and sentence she might have come up with (or should we say "down with"?) if, instead of good literature, all the language she absorbed came from cartoons or afternoon talk shows on television.

SEVEN

Language Modeling and Vocabulary Growth

Oral modeling is related directly to increasing the size of our vocabulary and building the sophistication of the syntax that will be available to us later as writers. Discussions of vocabulary growth often employ the pyramid shape to picture the relative sizes of different portions of our functional vocabulary. As we look at vocabulary development here, I want to use this pyramid but invert it so that it is more like a funnel. On the following page is a simple graphic of my "funnel of functional vocabulary development."

This diagram proposes that we do not have a single, holistic, and uniformly available vocabulary. Rather, each of us has four separate functional vocabularies within the whole that are not only different in size and function, but into which words enter and progress in a particular direction and order. Understanding this model is important as we move closer and closer to writing.

Our largest functional vocabulary comprises words whose meaning and use we understand when we *hear and see them spoken by another person.*

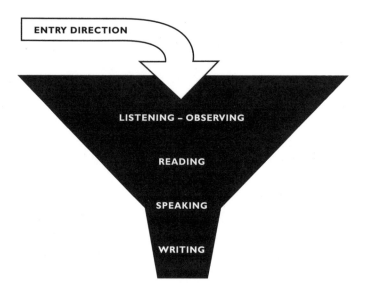

ENTRY DIRECTION

LISTENING – OBSERVING

READING

SPEAKING

WRITING

Listening and watching gives us such clues that we often understand new words instantly in this medium and incorporate them into the large first section of our partitioned vocabulary.

Next largest, but smaller than our "Listening-Observing Vocabulary," is that set of words whose meaning we understand when we *read them*. There are many words that we do not understand as we read them, but that, heard and watched in usage, would be clear. It is also true that words that are part of our reading vocabulary enter our total repertoire through the larger listening and watching door. It is unusual for children in the years of their early language growth process to add a new word directly at the reading stage, that is, by meeting it in reading when they have never heard it in use before. This may happen with a dedicated dictionary user, and it is often a usable growth process with more adult readers, but more often, the younger reader simply skips over an unknown word.

The third largest vocabulary section contains words that we ourselves call on *in our own oral and kinesthetic speech.* We do not use *all* the words we understand when others use them. Understanding does not make them "our words." In fact, much of what we hear and read never moves down into us enough to come out of our own mouths as our own speech.

Finally, the smallest vocabulary is that body of words that learning writers employ in their *writing.* When it comes to the written medium, usable vocabulary is often quite small in comparison to those words that we, in larger ways, can define and understand. When we write, we are choosing words from the very bottom, the smallest part, of our vocabulary funnel unless we are either accomplished writers or dedicated word lovers. Of all our vocabularies, it is the most limited for most learning writers.

Not only is the funnel metaphor usable to describe the diminishing numerical sizes of this four-tiered vocabulary, it is also usable in metaphorically describing the flow of words into those various tiers. Just as the funnel is open at its wide top, so we are usually most open to receiving new words into that widest and most open of vocabularies, that set of words we understand when we hear.

If the funnel metaphor works, what ends up below is a smaller and smaller portion of what is poured in at the top. The more often we see and hear that same new word used as we watch and listen, the more likely it is that we will eventually recognize it in our own reading. Having firmly accessed the new word through its being repeatedly modeled for us moves it more deeply down the funnel than does looking it up in the dictionary when we first come across it in our reading. Does anything more have to be said at this point about the value and function of storytelling and reading aloud in building that vocabulary we hope to use later on in writing?

This process continues as words move further down the funnel. In order for us to begin using a word in our own oral and kinesthetic speech, that word must already be in both our vocabularies of oral recognition and reading recognition.

In my own personal reading, I often return to re-read books that I remember reading years ago in childhood and adolescence. When I do this, I begin to see if I can discover why favorite remembered books fascinated me and why others, that I now enjoy in adulthood, did not captivate my imagination at all. This is usually done in some secret hope that the previously experienced magic will happen again and that new magic will be discovered.

During the last year, I revisited an eighth-grade favorite, Jules Verne's *Journey to the Center of the Earth*. With this new reading I was particularly struck by the frequent use of the word *savant* in connection with certain characters or acts of genius. While the word is one whose use and meaning I recognized without really thinking about it, I realized it was not a word I would likely use in my own speech and writing. I simply have not seen, heard, and read the word enough in my own listening and watching and reading to wiggle it on down my own narrowing funnel into personally usable vocabulary.

On the other hand, the old almost-exclusively musical term *segue* has recently been so prominently modeled in speech and print through its derivative form *segueway* that I have found myself, without thinking, using that very word both orally and in writing.

If our agenda is a rich writing vocabulary for ourselves or our students, it seems unlikely that we can achieve that richness by trying to squeeze new words directly into the bottom of the funnel. Rather, we must increase modeling from the top down. This means more listening, more being read to, more talking, more reading aloud, more personal reading, and not just more work directly at writing. Great musicians never stop listening to other musicians play. Great composers never stop playing music written by others. Good writers never stop listening to the stories of others or reading great works of literature. Even great basketball players love to watch other great basketball players play and to learn from such watching! Those who seek to be good writers must continue to pour words into their language funnel from its wide top so that more of those words will finally come out at the bottom.

A final word about dictionary and thesaurus work. Even the most dedicated dictionary and thesaurus user normally approaches these tools not as instruments for word *discovery* but rather as instruments for *clarification* and—in the case of the thesaurus—for remembering known but forgotten words. We look up words we have *already heard, seen, or read.* When we check the thesaurus, we choose from the options offered for a word we already do know but could not think of at the moment. It would be most unusual to choose from the thesaurus a word we have never seen or heard before, not knowing its specific meaning or its connotations. No, we use aids like the thesaurus to choose words we already know but could not think of when we needed them. Indeed, the cover copy of the thesaurus I use touts the book not as a catalogue of unknown and new words but as a tool to help one express thoughts with "precision, color, and variety."

Here is a real and practical example. I look up the word *common*. I am writing about the books that my wife and I both like to read, but when I look back at my sentence it says, "We share common enjoyment of a number of American novelists." When I see what I have written, I am afraid that someone may read the word *common* to mean "of mediocre quality." So, I turn to the thesaurus in search of a *word that I already know* but can't think of at the time in order to add precision and clarity to what I am writing.

Among the words offered as synonyms for *common* is the word *conjoint*. I do not choose this word since its specific meaning is unknown to me and it would not be a "normal" or comfortable word to come from either my mouth or my pen. Then I see another synonym: *mutual*. This, in terms of the sentence I am working on, seems to me to be the word that is both familiar and fits my needs. Now my sentence is more precise as it becomes, "We both share mutual enjoyment of a number of American novelists."

The dictionary and the thesaurus are like cookbooks for those whose pantries are already filled with groceries. They enable us to make good *choices*. However, neither the dictionary nor the thesaurus can put food on the table when there is nothing in the word pantry to begin with.

EIGHT

Let's Get on to Writing

So far we have covered the following topics related to understanding language and moving toward writing:

- A New Look at Teaching Language
- A New Look at Functional Language Development
- What is Language?
- Soaking Up Our Primary Language
- Building Visual Listening and Reading Skills
- Language Modeling and Vocabulary Growth

Assuming that we understand these things and are doing them, let us move on to building a writing curriculum model that reflects and encourages our most natural language growth. Here are step-by-step plans for such a model.

Writing: Our First Foreign Language

In the first half of this book, we spent much time looking at language acquisition. We tried to take apart and understand our most primary language—

that oral and kinesthetic package we absorb without realizing that we are learning anything.

As we come to writing, the metaphor we will employ is that of our first "foreign" language. Let us expand on this metaphor by looking at what we normally mean when we use the term "foreign" language.

No matter where in the world we live, our first language (be it French, Spanish, Swahili, or a Chinese dialect) is that language we absorb from our surroundings without any awareness of its absorption. A "foreign" language, by contrast, is something we are taught (even if self-taught) and are aware of being taught. Note that people who grow up in bilingual cultures may very well absorb more than one primary language, neither of which could be called either "foreign" or "second." The term "foreign," when we use it here with reference to language, means just that: secondary and learned deliberately.

It is with this meaning in mind that we speak here of *writing* itself as being a "foreign" language. Writing does not occur naturally or by absorption: we must be taught to write, and, as with any new language, writing remains "foreign" until we become bilingual.

Why use this metaphor for writing activity? *The reason is that when a language is foreign, it is not usable as a workable creative medium.* We simply do not create well in a foreign language.

When can we say that we have become bilingual

and that any languages we study no longer are "foreign" to us? The popular answer is, "When you start to dream in them..." Once we can dream, once we can *think*, once we can *create* in a foreign language, it is no longer foreign, but we have, in fact, become bilingual.

With regard to writing, once we can process our thoughts in writing as easily, as fluently, and with syntax and vocabulary as complex as we use in conversing, then we have become bilingual and can engage in "creative writing." The question for teacher and learner is: "How many sixth graders, how many high school seniors, how many forty-year-olds can actually create in writing as easily and as fluently as they can converse with a friend?"

It is for those who cannot so easily write that we are developing this writing model. Because it works from a base of oral and kinesthetic competence, there is also a second target group. There are rare students, some of whom are still in their elementary years, who do become quickly competent in written language. Some of these "easy writers," especially if they are shy, may begin to *prefer* writing to talking as their oral and kinesthetic skills stop growing or begin to wane. Who cannot think of brilliant friends who read and write their way through graduate school and then cannot simply explain their specialties? Because our model continually switches back and forth between the oral and the written, it may also prove useful in helping these easy writers remain fearlessly and competently grounded with oral and kinesthetic skills.

This is our operating principle: if writing is a foreign language for many of us, and if we do not create well in "foreign" languages, then we must step back into our most familiar "first" language as our creative medium. From this starting place, we must learn to "translate" into that new foreign language called writing. Once, working in our first language, we discover that we do have something worth writing about, then our desire to translate will increase.

In order to proceed concretely, we will choose a target group to build our writing model around. I have chosen a class of sixth-grade students who have Miss Smith as their teacher. What we will do is to build the model in its ideal form for this group with the realization that we may tune the process up or down to make the steps practical for writing groups ranging in ages from kindergartners to adults.

Miss Smith has a class of twenty-six students: fourteen girls and twelve boys. She teaches at Eastside Middle School in a small town that was once rural but now has become a commuting town less than an hour from the city. Her class is somewhat mixed racially, culturally, and economically, and it is a public school. Just as the details may differ for us, so our own plans will have to be adjusted.

Step One: Creating Writing Clubs

As we begin to build a writing model based on oral and kinesthetic language, it is important to remember the wholeness of our language. Since one of the main dimensions of our first language is the give-and-take and the powerful way in which a listener guides the communicator, it is essential that we create a way to take advantage of the creative richness of this language dimension. Trying to talk by yourself does not have the creative power of talking in a group with all its nourishing and corrective feedback.

The first thing we will do with Miss Smith's sixth graders is to divide them in units called "Writing Clubs."

Question: How large should the writing clubs be? As with many questions that will arise from this model, the answer is: "It depends."

In general, I would not want to work, as a teacher, with more than four groups even in a large class. The ideal group size is about six students. Since Miss Smith has twenty-six students in her class this year, we will put them into four clubs, two groups of six and two groups of seven.

In consulting on curriculum development, I work with schools of all types and sizes. In the past year alone, I have been in fifth-grade classes ranging from eleven to thirty-three students. On the high end of this model, that larger class would need four clubs with as many as eight or nine in a group. On the low end, the right classroom dynamic might even allow for a single unit, depending on the students' history of working together.

In kindergarten through college classes, dividing the students into small groups seems best. For adults, however, larger groups often work well. Even as I write, I have been working with an adult group of twenty-one members. They have strongly preferred to work together rather than being subdivided because, in their words, even though they do not get to talk as much individually in the larger group, they learn more from listening than they do from talking anyway. In short, they don't want to miss anything they might lose if they were not all functioning and working together.

With writing groups in school (such as in Miss Smith's sixth-grade class), I achieve a more cooperative spirit if I call the subdivisions not "groups" but rather "clubs." Their success is further enhanced if I have the students corporately name their clubs and even go to the extent (with care to age appropriateness) of having them engage in some group-building activities such as creating slogans, mottoes, poems, songs, or TV ads. Since we function better creatively when we are with people whom we know and like, there must even be occasional times for the "writing club" to engage in social activities.

Groups function well when two factors are in healthy balance. First, members must have a task that is understandable, doable, and clearly defined.

Second, they must be able to turn aside from that task and care for one another if the need arises. In Miss Smith's class, for example, if Janie comes to school having just learned that she has to move because of her mom's new job, or if Jack's dog died over the weekend, the club will write best if it knows how to pause first to care for people's personal needs.

Question: As the year moves on, do people stay in the same writing club? The answer is "Yes… but…" People should stay in the same groups long-term, but with an early provision for adjustment. When the year starts and Miss Smith gets her new class, she may not know them well enough to have an understanding of individual personalities. She may not yet know who is loud and who is quiet, who is shy and who is outgoing, who leads and who follows, or any and all of the other subtle dynamics that influence group interaction. In order to get groups that function well and with maximum compatibility, it is wise for her do two things: wait a few days before organizing the groups, then build in an automatic regrouping time after the first few weeks of observation. The adjustment solves problems caused by having all the talkers or all the nontalkers in the same unit. Once the groups are adjusted, it is important to keep them together as they progress through all the dynamics of family growth and bonding.

If Miss Smith's sixth graders are normal students, they may see their initial task as proving to her that this new thing she is trying will not work. After all, it is one of our jobs at every age to try to invalidate the plans and the wisdom of those who would teach us! Persevere! Sixth graders (of all ages) give up quickly when the teacher is determined. If this plan is to work, it will be as a long-term and repeatedly used model, not a one-time experiment.

Question: Do we work with all the groups at once, or with only one at a time? Again the answer is, "It depends." Some years, as a teacher, you may have a class so cooperative that all the writing clubs can be working independently without supervision. However, some years you may have one of those classes in which working with one group almost means locking the others up while you do it!

In the latter case, it may be wise to recruit "Writing Club Sponsors." They may be parents or other adults from the community (retired professional people may be quite excellent here) who could come into your class for only one hour a day each week to be with the writing club to which they are permanently assigned for the year. They may even take their club off to its own chosen work site, say in the school library or even out onto the school ground, and work with students outside their normal classroom. This possibility is especially important if all the writing clubs (with their sponsors) are working on their task at the same time.

The sponsor's role is neither to teach nor to lead but simply to be an adult member of the group, modeling and monitoring the task you give. This adult presence often does much for group maintenance. I encourage the adults to participate fully, actually trying out the same assignments the students have. Their modeling is invaluable in breaking stories loose through suggestion. With the sponsors in place, the teacher is set free to float from group to group, watching, enabling, and doing whatever policing might be necessary.

One final word about writing clubs. Did you ever stop to realize that creative writing is the only subject in school in which the *content* flow comes from the student to the teacher instead of the other way around? In other subjects (math, science, or history), the teacher is the initial holder of expert information—a reason we *change* teachers as we change levels in any academic field. No one teacher can "hold" and have readily accessible teaching plans for everything we are to be taught in mathematics at each level as we move from arithmetic through calculus.

This is not true of creative writing. The teacher's most effective role is not as information holder but as modeler and process enabler. Content in creative writing forever comes out of the mind and work of the student.

If this is true, then *why change writing teachers at every grade level?* Several of the best writing programs I have worked with are ones in which young writers continue to work with the same teacher more than a year. Following this model, imagine what would happen if, at the end of the year, Miss Smith gets a new class for all her other sixth-grade subjects but *keeps her writing groups for another full year*, while the usual eighth-grade teachers get a new group of sixth-grade writers and begin with them what is to be a three-year process.

Imagine the effectiveness of not having to start over, of teachers already knowing a great deal about individual strengths and weaknesses, of students being able to go back and pick up certain pieces of writing and follow them through two or even three years of development, reshaping and polishing.

In one middle school I have worked with for nearly ten years, the students actually spend all of the sixth, seventh, and eighth grades in the same writing group with the same teacher. The writing results I see in that school, both in student enjoyment of the process and in finished product, are outstanding. (By the way, that same school continues to score at the very top levels of all language test scores for the eighth grade.)

So, we have established, sponsored, and adjusted writing clubs in Miss Smith's sixth-grade classroom. Now what shall we do with them?

Step Two: Developing the Visual Story
Using our First Language

Earlier in this book we described a story as being a picture I see in my head that I would like for you to see. Let us pursue this image as we seek, through our groups, to unlock effective writing in Miss Smith's sixth-grade students.

If a story is, first of all, a picture I see in my head, this means that until I see a picture in my head, I have nothing to write. A great deal of the problem with writing, especially with young and inexperienced writers, is that they do not generate visual pictures or visualize experience in an active and deliberate pre-writing process. They waste time and paper without writing or internally "seeing" anything. No picture equals no story.

Once someone "sees" a story, half of the writing battle is won. Once I see that I have a story to begin with, I may become almost eager to learn how to save it in writing. Let's try to break down this dilemma.

Our brains are wonderful storage computers that record and save all the experiences of our lives. On the little hard disk in our head called human memory, our senses take in what we see, smell, hear, taste, and touch, as well as our interpretations of all these things. Our senses are like lenses on an infinitely competent camera that records the fullness of our life experiences.

The problem is that no one ever bothers to develop the film! When someone throws us into that foreign language we call writing and asks us to create something there, it is very much like handing someone a roll of undeveloped film and asking him to print pictures without going through the process of developing it.

We all know that we cannot print pictures from undeveloped film, no matter how wonderful are the experiences, people, and places caught in the shots. Neither can the writer for whom writing is still a foreign language move straight from unprocessed memory into writing without going through an intermediate process.

Under this writing model, we shall use our own natural oral and kinesthetic language to develop the unprocessed film rolled up in our memories. As we "see" the pictures in our imaginations, we may learn to "print the photographs"—that is, to move what we see into writing.

The reason we created the writing clubs in the first place was to have workable units for orally and kinesthetically processing our pre-writing, a step designed to create visual internal imagery for writing. Let us walk our way through the process.

On the first day that I meet with Miss Smith's sixth-grade writing clubs, I do not even talk about writing. In fact, I may not even begin to use that word yet. After all, I do not want the fears that may have built up through earlier years to interfere with what we are doing now.

All I am going to do is ask the students a question that will become the center of sharing and discussion (yes, talking!) in their writing clubs. The question I often use first on people of various ages is this: "Have any of you ever had a pet that you don't have anymore?" (This question and about sixty others come from an earlier book of mine, *Telling Your Own Stories* [August House, 1993].)

I say nothing at all about writing; I simply walk in and ask the question. Then, before anyone even has a chance to volunteer, I offer my own response as a model for what they might do themselves. I spend three or four minutes telling about my little bantam hen, "Banty"—starting with where I got the chicken, through its naming process, its description, and things I used to do with it, right on to its eventual demise.

I have deliberately chosen to tell them about a pet other than a dog or a cat. This is because the word *pet* may connote for them only dog or cat, and I want the students without either to think beyond this stereotype until they find memories of any sort of pet they once had.

The reason I model first is mostly to slow them down in their talking so that I don't get hurried responses like "I had and dog and it died...the end!" I model not content but descriptive process.

Once I have told about Banty, I stop to ask the students whether there is anything more about my pet they would like to know. I then take time to respond to their inquiries. This builds the story more and more visually as I fill them in on the things that I assumed everyone knew but which, of course, could not be known unless I specifically told about them.

Finally, I ask the original pet question again and check to see whether I have a volunteer who wishes to have us meet a pet.

In Miss Smith's sixth-grade class there are several students who always have their hands up before the question is completely out of the teacher's mouth. In making up the writing club groups, I want us to be sure that these easy volunteers do not all end up in the same group but rather that they are equally distributed among all the clubs. For now, in the group I am watching, Willie raises her hand and wants to tell us about Blackie.

For the next three and a half minutes we hear of when Willie was about to be seven years old and wanted a dog for her birthday. She lived in another town then and so she tells us a little bit about where she lived and why her parents didn't think their house was a good place for a dog.

Her "story" goes on through the convincing arguments to get the dog, the day it came home, the naming process, its bad smell when it got wet, several things Blackie liked to do, and things Willie liked to do with the dog.

Suddenly another group member, Bob, blurts out, "What happened to it?" and the story goes on. We hear about Blackie's talent for having babies and the family decision to have the dog neutered.

Then comes the final chapter in which poor Blackie is run over and killed just one day after coming home from the neutering stay at the animal hospital.

As soon as Willie has finished her portrait of Blackie, two other hands quickly go up as other students in the group are now ready and eager to have us meet their pets. In unhurried order we hear about Samuel's rabbit and then about Camika's pet iguana. By the time five students have introduced their pets, Carmine's hand goes up. We know that Carmine is the quietest boy in the class, the one who seldom offers any comment and never volunteers an answer to a question. However, after hearing about (and visualizing) all the other pets, he now has a memory of his own. "One time we were riding in the car and I saw this turtle crossing the road and I asked my mom if we could stop and get it and I could take it home and we did…" Carmine is on the way with the introduction of his own pet.

Let us look at several things that are happening.

First, when it is all over, we have only spent thirty minutes on this process, including my (or the teacher's) original pet story modeling at the beginning. This means that each student had used only about four minutes on average.

In normal human speech, we move words at a rate that ranges from 75 to 150 words per minute when we are thinking about what we are saying. On the other hand, when we write longhand (and think about what we are writing), it has been estimated that we move words only at the rate of 10 to 12 words per minute. This means that if Willie spent about three and a half minutes telling us about Blackie, she orally staked out a story of about 250 to 300 words, even with fairly slow-moving speech. Even if she could have written the story, and the probability is that she could not have, it would have taken a good thirty minutes of nonstop writing to do so.

The more important thing, though, is that while Willie was telling about Blackie, several important and creative dynamics were occurring not only with her but in the total group as members watched, listened, and responded.

In the first place, using her comfortable oral and kinesthetic language, she was developing some of the undeveloped film in her own head. All of the undeveloped "Blackie" film was developing in her visual memory as she gradually told us more and more about her pet. Once its development started, it was available to use later on for her writing. Also, once she began to develop this memory, it continued to develop even after she had told her little story. If she thought or even told about Blackie a week later, many more memories would have appeared during the intervening time.

Note that this processing medium is not "oral" but "oral and kinesthetic." That is, Willie could not have gone into an empty room with only a tape recorder and processed this same story in this way. No, the story is being partially pulled out of her by the faces of the others in her writing club who are watching and listening. Remember that listeners are like magnets that pull our stories from us. This is one of the primary reasons for processing in the clubs rather than trying to begin alone. In short, the feedback dynamic of our language is a good creative enabler when used in this way.

What are all the listeners doing while Willie is telling us about Blackie? They are, of course, thinking about their own pet memories and remembering more and more of what they will tell when their turn comes. In addition to content, they are, without even being aware of it, noting the shape and form of how she tells her story and either fitting their own material into that shape or modifying and expanding it for their own use.

Over time, as we try this process with different people going first, there is more and more learning from one another and more and more support and help for one another. There is also more and more appreciation for other group members as we meet them more fully through their stories.

There is one other advantage in this kind of initial processing. When we are writing and get stuck, we quit. Then, when we try to work again, we have to start all over and get back our emotional steam and our content consciousness. However, in oral and kinesthetic group processing, when we get stuck, the group keeps pulling the story out of us. There may even be questions like, "What happened after that?" The group will not let go until the listeners are satisfied with the story.

When we are writing, only one person is working on the story. Even if we rewrite it a hundred times, only one person is working on the story. But when we tell the story to six or seven other people whose faces are immediately giving us helpful editorial feedback, there are immediately six or seven people helping us with our creative process.

Question: Should there be feedback at this stage? If feedback means criticism, the answer is an overwhelming no. We are working here with newborn stories and, just like babies, newborns need no criticism. All that newborns need are food, love, and cleaning up! However, a very helpful followup question at this point may be: "Now that you've heard this much about Blackie, what other things would you like Willie to tell us about her?" This is a question that helps and nourishes her story because it says, "I like your baby...could I look at her some more?"

Finishing Step Two

After all the members of the group have told about their pets, what do we do to finish this step and begin to move on to the next? The answer depends on the age of the group and the individual language skills of the students involved.

With Miss Smith's sixth graders I would finish step one in this way: "OK, students. Weren't those great new stories you just heard? They were so good that I wish everyone could hear those stories. I wish you could tell those stories over and over until everyone in the *world* could hear them. I'll bet they would even get to be bigger stories if we got a chance to tell them over and over. Too bad we can't do that.

"Our time is almost up for today, but before we stop, let's do one thing. This is just for you, not to turn in and not for your teacher. You should save this, though, for your future writing file.

"Take about two minutes to write, in any way you want to, just enough *about* the story you told so that *you won't forget it.*"

At this point I want to push the students until they are actually trying to write more than I am giving them time to write. They are so accustomed to being given more time than they can fill with writing that I want to do the opposite. "We only have *two* minutes, so work as quickly as you can so that you can hang on to this story."

Part of what I am having them do, of course, is to think about which parts of the story they just told are the most essential. At the same time, they are discovering that they have more than two minutes' worth that they could write.

Question: What about my kindergartners or my English-as-a-Second-Language students? They can't even write a sentence! What do they do?

At this point I am interested in preserving the "film" the student developed in visual imagination, not in the final form in which it is stored. So, with younger students, with students for whom English itself is a primary barrier, with students who are simply better at *drawing* than at writing, the storage medium is simple: "Draw just enough so that you won't forget the story you told us." In fact, with older students like Miss Smith's sixth graders, we might even try to combine drawing (even stick figures and primitive cartoons) with writing.

Above all, we do not want the storage medium to become more important than the content of the story we are trying to save. We are not taking time for completed artwork any more than we are taking time for finished writing. All we want now is some proof of what happened and some primitive document that will call the story to mind.

What I *do* want at this time is the beginning of a writing folder kept by each member of each writing club. This is not to be graded or turned in except to give evidence that the job is being done. The folders may be stored at school so that they are always accessible to the students. They are quick documents created to hold the memory of the story processed orally.

For now, simply hold on to this primitive document.

Question: Do we move on to writing now? Not yet. First, I want us to repeat this basic step three to four times over a period of days or weeks before we go any farther. The next time we try this process, we will do so with a different prompt such as: "Did you ever break something that belonged to someone else?...Did you ever do something you had already been told not to do?... Did you ever try to cook something that didn't work?" I want to offer one prompt or concrete topic in question form, followed by enough time for each member of the club to talk his or her way through the picture it brings up in memory, followed by quick documentation for a folder. In case we have not been clear, each student and each club works with a single question each time.

Once we have done this three or four times, then we will move on to step three.

Step Three: Beginning to Learn to "Translate"

To this point, students in Miss Smith's class have spent four sessions over a three-week period "talking" stories into visual existence. They have worked in their primary oral and kinesthetic language to develop some of the undeveloped film inside their heads. They also have stored personal and minimal "notes" to keep them from forgetting about the story they gave birth to. These notes they are keeping in their own personal files for later use.

Now it is time to move from this oral and kinesthetic beginning place toward learning to "translate" what they have done into a piece of acceptable writing.

Question: Why have we gone through the oral/kinesthetic process four times before getting on toward writing? The reason goes back to a teacher (she shall remain unnamed) whom I once had in upper-elementary school. The year that I was in her room we would attempt to write stories and were always met with the same comment from her when she read our initial work: "That writing would be good if you would work on it more!"

I soon came to know that a great deal of my writing would never be better even if I worked on it until the end of the world. The reason for this was my realization that a great deal of my writing fell into the category called "a bad start." When you have made a bad start, the most helpful thing is not to keep working on what is broken but rather to make a new start.

When working with Miss Smith's sixth graders, we quickly learn that *the more concrete the question, the better results we get.* "Tell me about a time you tried to cook something that didn't quite work" produces much better and clearer results than "Tell me about a time you got into trouble." The backside of concreteness is, however, the possibility that not all students have had specific experiences to connect with. If our prompt was "Tell us about a pet you once had that you don't have anymore," there may be a person in our group who has truly never had a pet.

If I moved immediately from the first experience of oral and kinesthetic processing into writing, I would be pushing some of the group members to

work on bad starts pointlessly. Nothing is as dis-
couraging as being pushed to keep working on
something that you very well know is bad.

What if you were learning to carve small
wooden animals, and the piece of wood you were
working on split almost as soon as you were getting started? You should, of course, toss it out and
start over on a new piece of wood. You would not
expect to be told to keep carving on the broken
piece, and to even proceed to sand and finish it
before you threw it out. No, time would be much
better spent by starting over.

I want us to do the same thing with writing;
therefore, this model has within it a time at the
very beginning when students are commissioned
to discard their bad starts.

At this point, we have made four starts with
Miss Smith's writing groups. Out of the four, each
student may have a bad start or two. That is completely normal! We have not all had the same experiences, and we cannot all be equally creative
about every subject that comes along. Therefore,
we make multiple starts so that we can discard bad
ones and then feel good about what we are moving forward with.

My instruction to the students now becomes:
"Look at your folders. You have in them some
notes from four different times when we have
talked in our groups. Look at what you wrote or
drew to help you remember your stories. Now,
from those four stories that you have already told

us about, I want you to pick the one that you think is the *very best and the most worth working on* as a story." What I am doing is deliberately allowing all the students to discard their weakest starts and pick something they think is strong enough to warrant working on.

After looking at all her "notes," Willie decides that what she told about her dog "Blackie" is the best of all the stories she has worked with so far. She picks it as the story she wants to keep working on. Other students in Miss Smith's class look over their own notes and do the same.

Now we begin to translate. My goal is to help people take the story that already exists in their heads (they "created" it through oral and kinesthetic telling, and it has continued to live and work on its own since that initial telling) and move it into the documentation medium we call "writing." This may take several tries while the teacher works to help each student find what works for him or her.

This is the first process we might try: "Remember that all of you told some really great stories and that you have each picked your very best one. Now you already have the story. You created it and worked on it when you told us about it, and it may even be that you've remembered more since you first told about it. All I want you to try is this: Could you try to write out every single thing that you have already told us about?"

For some people that is enough. I have seen

many students take this directive and move a story that took four minutes to tell directly into six hundred words of writing even when they had never been able to do what had been called "creative writing" before. Hurrah when that works…we will pick these students back up at our next level of writing development. For some others, however, we need to do more work now.

Sometimes it is difficult for students to move in a wholesale way from their visual memory into full-scale writing. When this is true, we need to find some ways to help them inch into the water that they cannot yet dive into. Here follow several processes that have proved to be workable.

I look at Sallie's "notes" and discover that she wrote five sentences about the time she tried to cook breakfast for her grandmother's birthday and almost burned grandma's house down. She can't seem to get started. To get her going, I have her take five sheets of paper (one for each sentence she wrote). Then I have her take the five sentences she wrote in her "notes" and rewrite one of these sentences in the center of each of the five sheets of paper. If the sentences she wrote were not in chronological order (with respect to the flow of the story), I now have her put them in that order. Once they are in chronological order, I have Sallie look at them with these guidelines: "Sallie, look at the sentence on your first sheet of paper. Can you think of anything you told us that happened *before* what you wrote about in that first sentence?" In only a moment Sallie has thought not just of one thing but of two things that come before the first sentence in her "notes." Not only that, she suggests that she has even remembered something else since she told the story to her club. She writes all these things down, and we are on the way.

With this format, what we do is ask Sallie to look at her original sentences, think of the things that happened between each, and simply write down what she thinks of. If we had not done the original oral processing that this model is based on, Sallie would have nothing to "think about" but would still be trying to create in a foreign language. Since she has already done the creative job in the earlier telling, her job here is a combination of remembering, enhancing, and documenting, not creating.

Let me share one other way of getting into documentation that I did not invent but that was offered to me by a fifth-grade student at a school in Connecticut. The teacher had been using the present model for some time when one of her students showed her how he "really did it" when working on his writing at home. She asked him to share his invention with me, and with their permission, I pass it on.

Jack had told a story in his writing club and had then written a six-sentence plot summary and put it in his notes. This particular story was about a trip he had taken with his family that he never wanted to take again. Three weeks after his original telling, it was this very story that he decided was his best work, and he wanted to move it into writing.

To show me how he did this, Jack went to his desk and came back with a rolled-up piece of paper that looked something like a homemade scroll. Suddenly he let go of the "scroll" as he held onto one end, and down to the floor unrolled a series of taped-together sheets of paper making one joined piece about six feet long. Then Jack showed me what worked for him.

He had put these pieces of paper together and had turned them so that they made a long horizontal sheet. Then he had copied his six-sentence plot summary in a single line across the top of the long paper from left to right.

After that Jack had looked not only at each sentence but also at the words within the sentences. Every time he could think of something he had told about but had not written, he would draw a line from where that part should fit into the story and jot it down in the open space below. When he had done this until all his thoughts were exhausted, Jack then copied the story out in proper linear (chronological) order. It worked for him like magic.

The point is that there is no unbendable and sacred process. The real secret is to find some way that works concretely to enable each student to "translate" what has already been told into the written medium.

Once students have found a way that works for

them and are sure they have written everything they told earlier, we are ready for the next stage.

Step Four: Enhancing the Initial Written Story

Note that so far we have paid no attention to "form" considerations such as spelling, punctuation, and grammar. At this point our interest is still content, not final form. Using our wood-carving analogy, spelling and punctuation are the equivalent of sanding and finishing. We do not really turn to them until we have completed the basic content part of the carving. Later on, of course, we will, through practice, become aware that attention to such details early in the process makes final sanding and finishing a much easier task. Just as it is easier to sand off a tiny burr than to use sandpaper to remove a whole section of wood, it is easier to come to final editing if every other word is not misspelled. For now, however, our interest is mainly content.

A time will come when Miss Smith's students are ready to swear that they have accomplished their task. They will come to that point when they are convinced (and are working to convince Miss Smith) that they have, in fact, written down every single thing that was originally told in the formative oral and kinesthetic version of the story and lots of new things besides. Well and good. Instead of arguing, let's go on from there.

At this stage it is helpful to remember that the original oral telling did not happen in a vacuum.

No, there were six other people who heard Willie tell about her dog "Blackie." Therefore, there are six usable memories to help her glean content for her story.

We remember that if a writer is working alone, there may be no source of outside aid until the book finally goes to the editor. In this case the writing may be revised or rewritten a hundred times and it is still the creative product of a single person. However, when Willie told her story to the six other people in her group, six instant helpful contributors to the life and content of her story were created. Let us take advantage of that reality.

At this point, I put Miss Smith's students back into their writing clubs with the stories they have now written as they sought to translate what was told onto paper. Then I have them exchange their written stories.

Remember that as each person sees someone else's work, he or she is reading a story heard before. As this reading proceeds, I ask the students to keep two questions in mind: What about the story you are reading is really good and you really like? What things do you remember about this story when you heard it told that you do not yet see written here?

Note that these are not negative questions. Rather, they are designed to prompt the further growth of a story's content. Sometimes the most obvious part of the story does not get told because it is so close to the teller. For this reason, the first two questions may now be followed by a third: What in this story would you like to hear more about?

After these questions are considered, then students take their own stories back, get the helpful feedback, and "fatten" the written story more. The word *fatten* is useful at this point. We want to make the story bigger, not longer. The word *longer* implies that we are adding more to the end of the story. But we are not doing that; rather, we are adding more at various places inside the story all along the way.

In order to fatten, we need to have the story in some format that will accept more weight. Margins wide enough for lots of note making, with arrows indicating the places where the "fat" goes, will work well. So will extra spaces between paragraphs. I simply want to be sure that the story in its first full written form has enough open space to accept many notes and jottings related to new additions.

There are several variations on how much to use this particular step before moving on. On some occasions, Miss Smith has students exchange stories only one time and then rewrite them with additions and changes. At other times, there may be a series of exchanges and rewrites, even carried on to the extent of having the entire group hear the story together again and give feedback. Above all, Miss Smith will try to keep the overall model fresh and avoid repetitiveness.

This time when someone finally thinks that he or she has written all there is to write, I try one more step. I will ask the student to read through the story that has been written, then put it down and tell it again as well as it can be told. Almost without exception the student will, in the telling, add new material in response to listening faces in the audience. At this stage it may be helpful to have students tell their stories either to the entire class or to a different writing club from their own so that they may have fresh listeners to look back at them as they tell.

Please note that we keep moving back and forth, back and forth between writing and telling, writing and telling. This builds the content and shape of the written story and, at the same time, boosts the quality of oral communication, something we often spend little time doing in school. It also removes writing from being a secretive, private endeavor by opening up the process to helpful observation from the beginning. The modeling of the teacher is critical with regard to this latter point. Only when we as teachers are willing to share our own imperfect efforts do we inspire our students to let go of their fears and bring their own writing efforts out into the nourishing light of day.

To this point, we have worked with Miss Smith's sixth graders from three to five weeks, depending on how much emphasis and time she is putting on the writing agenda. During that time, we have watched the initial creation of four beginning place stories as they were given birth in the oral and kinesthetic medium. Then we have watched while one of those stories was chosen as best and "translated" into writing. The result is a fairly completely written story. We have still, however, not attended to matters of grammar, spelling, and punctuation. Where do we go now?

What we do now is actually to keep in our writing files what we have done thus far, and then go back and start all over again to find a new story and bring it up to this level. At this point I still may not have students with work worth sanding and finishing, so I do not want them to waste their time and energy trying to do those two tasks until we have the right thing to work on.

So, we begin the same process all over. Go back to the writing clubs and launch a new series of "starts" with additional prompts. This time our first question might be: "Have you ever known someone you wish every person in this class could meet? Tell us about him or her." (See Appendix B for an extensive list of writing club prompts.) Again we follow the same process, except that Miss Smith's students are getting better and better at it! Again after four starts we move into the "translation" process, which is pushed until we have all the content we can get. After the new written story is taken as far as possible, I have the students file it and start all over yet again.

After we have about three fully written stories (which could take from nine to fifteen weeks, depending on how rapidly I push this process), we will move to the next level.

Step Five: Moving Toward Publication

Incentive is one of the most important keys to working with writers of any age. As we deal with those mechanical matters of spelling, punctuation, and other aspects of grammar, how do we offer enough incentive to make the effort work, even make it joyous and interesting? The key is found in establishing a purpose for all of this work. The purpose is called "publication."

What does the term mean? Basically, it means that what is being written is not for the writer but for a "consumer"—that is, someone who will read what we have written and, in fact, is the person we are writing for to begin with.

This is very different from journaling, which is essentially writing to and for yourself. When you are keeping a journal, it is easy to develop various forms of "shorthand" that you use because you know what you mean by them even though no one else does. In journaling it does not matter because the writing is for your own eyes anyway.

It is easy for young writers to fall into this mode of writing, especially if journaling exercises have been part of school work for some time already. There is really no concern given to spelling and punctuation because the reader, who is also the writer, can decode his or her own shorthand.

Publication requires a reversal of mindset from self-focused writing to reaching another target reader. The very realization that "someone whom I do not know is actually going to read what I have written" is, in itself, often a huge motivator toward cleaning up one's written language. Let us look at several versions of publication that Miss Smith's sixth-grade class could try.

Publication may be putting together a particular set of stories from Miss Smith's class, binding it, and placing it in the school library where other students and teachers *from now on and forever* may continue to find it and check it out. Publication may be putting together a set of stories, binding them, and presenting them to the residents of a retirement home nearby so that they can see the kinds of things Miss Smith's students are writing about (and perhaps later share some of their own stories). Publication may involve creating a class mailing list of relatives (grandma and grandpa), friends, school officials, and other community leaders and then, a couple of times each year, sending them a set of stories perfected by the class.

In one North Carolina school I was in, kindergartners and first graders had made up a class mailing list and sent mailings to all the people on their list several times during the year. It was a great thrill to all of these students to know that there was a vehicle for their creative thought and work. They were proud and, at the same time, a bit nervous when they realized that their grandmother was on the mailing list and she would read the very story they had written in class.

Here is another stopping point. After three full-of-content stories have been written down, however crudely, during the first nine to fifteen weeks of trying this model in the classroom, Miss Smith will pick one of those three (one from each student's work) that she can honestly praise as being the best work he or she has done since starting this method of writing. She can praise it for, out of the nine to fifteen tries to make a start, this comes the closest to what she would hope her students might achieve. One reason for finally choosing a story to work on to the finishing point is that when Miss Smith tells the student that this particular story is worth working on, she is believable. Telling students that *everything* they begin to write is worth working on is not credible to them, and it is not true. However, by the time we have worked up the pyramid from multiple starts to this point, Miss Smith's honest praise is believable.

Now it is time to go to the class with the teacher's selected stories, one for each student to push to perfection, with the assurance that they are worth publishing…if we can get them cleaned up in time! At last we have moved all the way to writing, with the assumption that some stranger will read Bobby's story and may love it, dislike it, or even criticize it.

The next step is simple. We will have the students imagine that their story is to be read by someone with the following characteristics: Their reader has never met the writer and does not know a thing about him or her—not the person's sex, age, or personality. Their reader has never been to where the writer lives, nor to where the story takes place if it is at a different place from where the writer lives. Their reader is both of a different age and different sex than the writer. (It may even be helpful at times to imagine the reader coming from a different country and having a different racial, regional, or ethnic background.)

I want our writers to assume nothing about the work their readers will do in trying to understand what has been written. I want to build an awareness that in clear writing we have to "tell all" in order to paint the picture fully. If we have a problem with the rare student who writes too much, hurrah! That is a much easier problem than what we usually find.

Another thing that I want to do at the level of preparing for publication is to reward risk-taking so that writing becomes richer and more complex. When students are afraid of getting "red marks" on their papers, they will often drop back to a writing level far below their oral-language level because they can't spell all the words that they speak or punctuate the complex sentence that rolls easily off their tongues. I do not want Miss Smith's sixth graders to write like fourth graders in order to avoid red marks on their papers, so I want us to *reward* rather than *punish* risk-taking. I want them to have a reason for trying to pull words from their larger vocabularies of listening and speaking into their usable vocabulary for writing.

How do we do this? Here is one simple example. I tell the student that if he or she knows a word but is not sure of the spelling, to use it anyway and *underline* the uncertainty. My response is to reward the writer for taking a risk and let him or her know whether the word is spelled or used correctly, or whether some fine tuning is needed in either case. I do the same with punctuation, syntax, and other grammatical mysteries, crediting the risk and talking about the usage to affirm or fine tune.

"Won't they just underline everything?" one teacher asked. Maybe so, but if students know that underlined elements have to be discussed, they gradually arrive at a reasonable balance.

Before this final publication-preparation process is finished, I again want to get help from Miss Smith's writing clubs. The final step before last draft writing is to read each other's stories. The exchanges should not pair the same students as were paired when we did this earlier because now I want a fresh reader for each piece.

The new reader's question could be something like this: "What if your grandmother were reading this story...what are the parts that she would not clearly understand?" With this helpful feedback, we now have students produce their final version of the story, to be published in a hard-copy form that may be read by anyone who is interested. As we come to the publication level two or three times each year, these final questions could become more varied and more complex. An extreme version might even be: "Imagine that a being from another planet found this story and took it back to that planet. Would beings who had never been to earth understand the story and be able to visualize the pictures?"

I have been amazed in some classes by how many students want to read *all* the stories their friends have written. What better affirmation could a young writer have?

NINE

Final Connections and Considerations

What I have hoped to do in this book about language and writing is to build a process that eases into writing as a natural and enjoyable final stage in our language development without freezing our growth in that oral and kinesthetic medium we use every day, whether we are practicing medicine, repairing cars, or teaching school. I believe this process keeps together the wholeness of our language rather than treating writing as some compartmentalized specialty that can be dealt with apart from observing, listening, and speaking.

In the end, the most important thing about this writing model is that it is not a quick, try-it-one-time approach. It works best over a long enough period that students come to understand the over-all process itself. Why, as teachers, would we *not* want young writers as insiders in this educational adventure?

Let me again state that we cannot under-estimate the importance of modeling in the learning process. The most effective, interesting, and exciting writing students I meet are those whose teachers take the risk of telling their own stories and sharing their own flawed attempts at writing. Imagine the learning that takes place with the student who hears my story and then says to herself, "I think I can do better!"

That is something any language teacher should be pleased to hear.

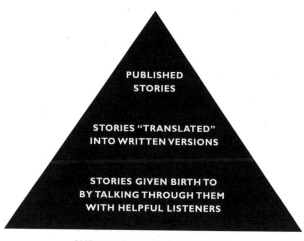

WRITING MODEL PYRAMID

Some Read-Aloud Stories for All Ages

There is a world of good read-aloud literature easily available for young children. There is also plenty of usable material available for elementary and older students. The latter material is, however, sometimes more difficult to locate. For purposes of example, the following list consists of the stories in my own August House collections.

The minimum grade levels given are those suggested to me by teachers and librarians who regularly use my work in their own read-aloud programs. Parents or teachers should, of course, read the stories for themselves first in order to check particular appropriateness for their own group of children or students. Some of these stories have been used with children much younger than those ages suggested, and some have been held back for older children's use.

In many cases, no upper age limit is given. These particular stories can be used from the minimum grade level shown through adult listeners.

Listening for the Crack of Dawn
Aunt Laura and the Crack of Dawn—4+
Winning and Losing—2+
Miss Annie—4+
The Last Butler in Sulpher Springs—6+
Christmas in Sulpher Springs—2+
Miss Daisy—4+
Dr. York—2+
L S / M F T—6+
The Haint—4+
Wild Harry—6+
Experience—8+
Daff-knee Garlic and the Great Drive-In Fire—8+
Winning and Losing…Again—8+
A Different Drummer—high school

Barking at a Fox-Fur Coat
Rainy Weather—4+
Uncle Frank and the Southern Bells—6+
Uncle Frank Saves the Jollys—6+
Whatever Happened to the Jollys?—6+
Jolly Old Saint Nicholas—6+
Uncle Frank Invents the Electron Microphone—6+
Uncle Frank Learns to Speak Polish—6+
Uncle Frank and the Crown Feed Boys—4+
Uncle Frank Cleans Up the Post Office—4+
Uncle Frank Almost Becomes a Detective—4+
Little Buchanan Outruns the Law—4+
Uncle Frank and the Snake Guineas—4+
Uncle Frank and the Talking Cat—4+
Aunt Esther and the Missing Cats—2+
Uncle Gudger's First Pet—4+
How to Get Rid of an Overfed Cat—4+
Old Man Hawkin's Lucky Day—2+

See Rock City

The Place—6+
Mrs. Rosemary—K-1 with care; 2+
Taking Care of the Bank—4+
Party People—K-1 with care; 2+
Dr. Franklin—4+
Tonsils—4+
See Rock City—4+
Beverly Davidson...Love from Afar—6+
Everybody Goes to the Beach—6+
Stanley, the Easter Bunny—6+
Walking Through Sulpher Springs—6+

Southern Jack Tales

The Time Jack Went to Seek His Fortune—2-6
The Time Jack Told a Big Tale—K-5
The Time Jack Got His First Job—K-5
The Time Jack Fooled the Miller—6+
The Time Jack Cured the Doctor—6+
The Time Jack Got the Silver Sword—2-6
The Time Jack Learned about Old and New—2+
The Time Jack Stole the Cows—K-5
The Time Jack Helped the King Catch His Girls—4+
The Time Jack Got the Wishing Ring—K-5
The Time Jack Solved the Hardest Riddle—6+
The Time Jack Went Up in the Big Tree—6+
The First Time Jack Came to America—6+

Other Donald Davis books

Thirteen Miles from Suncrest (a novel)—Grade 4+
Jack and the Animals (a picture book)—Age 3-8
Telling Your Own Stories (on writing)—Grade 4+

Questions and Prompts to Elicit Writing Ideas

My book *Telling Your Own Stories* (August House, 1993) lists a number of writing prompts and questions. For readers of this book, I now offer more.

The prompts are divided in four sections: First come "trouble" prompts that are basically *plot* related. Then follow *character*-related "person" prompts, *setting*-related "place" prompts, and finally a fiction-based-on-reality set of "speculation" prompts.

These sample prompts should not be used as replacements for your own original and creative story starters. They are offered here simply as models for the kinds of questions that often help people find stories hiding inside themselves.

Trouble Prompts (Plot):

1. Have you ever had to move from the place where you lived when it was not your idea?

2. Have you ever taught someone (maybe a brother or sister) to do something that you knew you shouldn't teach him or her? Did anyone ever do this to you?

3. Did you ever get hurt or lost or break something while doing what you already knew you were not supposed to do?

4. Did you ever go somewhere that you had already been told not to go?

5. Did an adult or someone else whom you trusted ever lie to you?

6. Did you ever do something that you later tried to avoid the blame for doing?

7. Did you ever try to run from your mother?

8. Did you ever make one of your parents (or even a teacher) so mad that it seemed as if steam might come out of his or her ears?

9. Have you ever found any money (or been with someone who did), and what did you then do with it? Have you ever lost any money?

10. Have you ever had a hobby that you wish could be your job?

11. Have you ever had to stay home by yourself when you were sick? While alone, did you do anything that you knew you weren't supposed to do?

12. Have you ever given someone else a present that you really wanted to keep for yourself?

13. Have you ever had someone steal something from you or from your home?

14. Did you ever get sick riding a carnival ride, seeing a movie, or taking a trip in a car, boat, or airplane?

15. Is there something that you were afraid of when you were little that you can laugh about now that you are older?

Person Prompts (Character):

1. Did you ever have a best friend who moved away? Help us meet that person and tell what happened after he or she was gone.

2. When you were younger, did you have a grandparent who changed or died? Can you help us meet that person as you knew him or her back then?

3. Did you ever meet someone at summer camp or on vacation whom you wish lived near you? Tell us all about meeting that person.

4. If you could disguise yourself as someone else, who would it be, and what would you do while you were in this disguise? (Try this idea disguised as a local person as well as someone famous.)

5. Have you ever had an adult friend you called by his or her first name even when you were very young? Help us meet this person.

6. If you could not live with your present family, tell us about the relative or friend you would most like to live with.

7. If one of your relatives had to come to live with you, tell all about the one you wish it could be. Or tell us about the one you hope it *wouldn't* be.

8. Tell us about either the person who taught you to ride a bicycle or the person who taught you to swim (or the person who taught you something else very important).

9. Have you ever known anyone of any age who had very unique hair (or maybe even no hair at all)? Help us to meet this person.

10. Have you ever met someone who didn't turn out to look the way you thought he or she would before you met the person?

11. Have you ever become friends with someone and later learned that he or she was famous or very talented in a way that you never imagined?

12. If you could spend one thousand dollars to do something for one of your parents, what would it be? Be sure that we meet the parent so that we understand your gift.

Place Prompts (Setting):

1. Can you take us with you to your favorite childhood picnic place and take us through your favorite things to do in that place?

2. What place do you know that would make a perfect hideout? Tell about the place and how you would fix it to be a hideout.

3. Tell us about your own house on Halloween (or any other holiday that you choose) if you had enough money to decorate it any way you pleased.

4. Tell us about a place you once went after your parents had already told you not to go there.

5. If you were to live on a farm, tell us about what kind of farm it would be and what you would grow or do there. (Try the same idea with an apartment in a city.)

6. If you inherited some land, tell us where in all the world you would want it to be, what it would be like there, and what you would do with it.

7. If you had to plan a one-day trip for a class of sixth graders, where would you take them and what would you do there?

8. If you could build one new room onto your house, what kind of room would it be and what would you put in it?

9. If you could design a perfect transportation vehicle, exactly what would it be like and how would it meet your needs and your dreams?

10. Where have you been that you would like to put a Hard Rock Cafe? Why?

Speculative Prompts
(Fiction based on Reality):

1. What if, for some reason, you were told that your school (or the place where you work) would be closed for the next full year. How would you spend this year? (It may be helpful to add a budget to this prompt or to say that money is no object!)

2. Suppose you woke up tomorrow to find that you had completely different hair in color, style, and texture from your real hair. Would you find some excuse to stay home, and if so, what excuse? Would you go to school (or to work) and create a story about what happened to your hair?

3. What if your favorite teacher had terrible breath or a problem with body odor? You are afraid to tell him or her outright, so how can you and your classmates make a plan to help your teacher?

4. If you were hired to be a bush teacher in the tundra of northern Alaska, what would you take to help with your teaching?

5. If you could start a business while you were still in high school (or even before), what kind of business might it be and how would you run it while finishing school?

Seen and heard on CNN, *Nightline,* and American Public Radio's *Good Evening,* DONALD DAVIS has also told stories for audiences throughout the U.S. and in the British Isles, New Zealand, and Indonesia. His other books include a novel, a children's picture book, two collections of stories, and two instructional books on writing and storytelling. An award-winning recording artist, he has received the Parents' Choice Gold Award, *Audiofile's* Earphones Award, *Storytelling World's* Best Audiotape Award, and a Notable citation from the American Library Association. He lives on Ocracoke Island off the North Carolina coast.